A guide to

GHOST WRITING

How To Sustain Manage And Build your
Brand As a Ghost Writer

By

Linda M. Valletta

TABLE OF CONTENTS

INTRODUCTION

I began my career with a love of stories and a desire
to succeed. I went on a roller-coaster ride with
unyielding determination, confronting both
triumphs and obstacles that would mold my fate.
Years ago, I discovered my talent for penning
engaging stories that affected readers' emotions. As
I delved more into Ghostwriting, my writings
brought numerous people's imaginations to life,
making them laugh, cry, and contemplate on life's
beauties.

Early on, I came upon an opportunity to write
for a well-known author, and I signed a contract
that seemed to be just what I needed. However, the
project fell through, leaving me heartbroken and
coping with the realities of the writing industry's
erratic nature. The ordeal was tough, but it only
spurred my determination. Debt became an
unwelcome companion as I engaged in my
profession, acquiring writing courses, attending

seminars, and putting money into marketing to advance my career.

The financial strain was heavy, but I remained determined, knowing that success often demanded sacrifices. I grew stronger and more stubborn with each rejection, honing my talents and learning from each failure. I recognized that adaptability was essential for survival in the ever-changing world of writing. My ambition to succeed became a driving force that propelled me ahead even through the darkest days. As my ghostwriting profession took off, I found myself working with powerful people, generating stories for celebrities and thought leaders. Each new endeavor presented its own set of obstacles and pleasures, reminding me of the diversity of the human experience.

Despite the flashes of accomplishment, there were times when self-doubt crept in. I doubted my worth as a writer and worried that my words would be insufficient. But, with the help of other authors and the acknowledgment of my clientele, I was able to silence my inner critics and embrace my skill.

As I worked to hone my trade, the debts that had previously troubled me began to fade. My investment in myself and my profession had finally paid off, and my hard work had been rewarded with financial stability. Knowing that my determination had led me to this point gave me an immense sense of success.

I eventually became a mentor for budding ghostwriters, passing on what I had learned over the years. I shared my experiences, including the highs and lows, to motivate people to pursue their objectives with zeal. I understood that success was more than just monetary gain it was also about assisting others in reaching their full potential. Today, I am a professional ghostwriter, having conquered various challenges along the way. My inspiring stories have touched many lives and left a lasting impression on readers all around the world. And in every article I write, I incorporate the lessons I've learned—the necessity of perseverance, the power of words, and the importance of remaining true to oneself.

I offer these words of advice to individuals seeking success in the field of ghostwriting: embrace your passion, embrace the hurdles, and never give up on your aspirations. The road may be difficult, but with perseverance, resilience, and a passion for writing, you, too, may find success as a ghostwriter and tell stories that touch people's hearts.

CHAPTER 1

AN OVERVIEW OF GHOSTWRITING

What exactly is ghostwriting? Writing copy in someone else's name is known as "ghostwriting." For example, as a freelancer, you might be requested to write a blog item and have it published under the CMO's name. (The "CMO's name" refers to the entire name of the Chief Marketing Officer (CMO) for whom the content is being written; the CMO's full name should be used as the author's name in the byline when a ghostwriter is hired to produce a blog post or any other piece of content that will be published under the CMO's name. As an illustration, if the CMO's name is Peter Chris and you authored a blog post for them as a ghostwriter, the byline on the finalized piece would read "Peter Chris ." This means that, despite the fact that you wrote the piece, the general public believes the CMO, Peter Chris , is the author.) In essence, ghostwriting is when another person's name appears next to yours on an article you created.

THE TRUTH ABOUT GHOSTWRITING

"I hear it's a terrific book," Ronald Reagan once said of his autobiography. "One of these days, I'm going to read it myself." It's unusual for a celebrity to be so open about their collaboration with a ghostwriter. The entire technique of ghostwriting appears shrouded in mystery. We're addressing some of the most frequent queries about the procedure in an effort to dispel the misconceptions and rumors around it:

What exactly is a ghostwriter? The term is defined as "one who writes for and gives credit of authorship to another" by the Free Dictionary, while the Oxford Dictionary defines it as "a person whose duty it is to write stuff for another author." Scribes penned stuff for kings in the 5th century B.C., and the practice dates back to that time. World leaders have used ghostwriters to present a favourable picture to their supporters throughout history. Even the venerable George Washington entrusted Alexander Hamilton with the composition of his Farewell Address. Christy Walsh, widely regarded as America's first sports agent, coined the phrase in 1921 when searching for ghostwriters to write autobiographies for sports figures such as Babe Ruth. Walsh was open about his use of ghostwriters, saying famously, "Don't insult the intelligence of the public by claiming these men write their own stuff." However, for many years, the practice was generally kept hidden from the publishing world.

Today, electronic publishing choices have reduced the cost of producing a book or other works. Celebrity autobiographies, combined with the rise of electronic media, have become an industry standard, increasing demand for ghostwriting assistance.

Who employs ghostwriters? Busy professionals frequently do not have the time to devote to a lengthy writing job. While many people love journaling or sharing ideas on social media as a creative outlet, they may lack the professional polish required for specific publications. A creative thinker works effectively with a ghostwriter in these situations.

Ghostwriters are used by politicians, celebrities, corporate executives, and even family historians.

Ghostwriters specialize in more than just memoirs and works of fiction. Blogs, thought leadership articles, speeches, scripts, ebooks, Wikipedia pages, music lyrics, op-eds, and editorial content are also among the projects they work on.

A few common misconceptions about ghostwriting? (Myths)

Because of its odd moniker, the ghostwriter industry is fraught with mystery and confusion. Among the most common myths are:

- Ghostwriters are difficult to locate - With thorough investigation, you should be able to identify a ghostwriter who is experienced in your subject area.

- Ghostwriters operate on commission - Most ghostwriters charge a flat rate and are willing to discuss payment arrangements before beginning work on your project.

- Any writer can ghostwrite well - it takes a unique skill set to complete the necessary research, provide customer service, and write convincingly in someone else's voice. Many well-known authors fail miserably as ghostwriters.

- Ghostwriters don't want credit: A prevalent misconception is that ghostwriters don't want credit for their work. While ghostwriters rarely earn public acclaim for their efforts, they do appreciate professional acknowledgment and respect, especially when working with prominent clientele.

- Some people argue that ghostwriting is dishonest or immoral because it entails someone else taking credit for the writing. However, ghostwriting is a legal service that is performed with the author's or client's full knowledge and consent. It is a collaborative process in which the ghostwriter translates the author's thoughts and vision into written content.

- Ghostwriters are mysterious and "ghost-like": The name "ghostwriter" conjures up ideas of shadowy beings lurking in the background. In actuality, ghostwriters are experienced writers who collaborate openly with customers to understand their requirements and provide a high-quality copy.

- While book ghostwriting is well-known, ghostwriters also work on a variety of assignments such as articles, blog posts, speeches, social media material, white papers, and more. They can help with various forms of writing to meet the needs of diverse clients.

- Some people believe that hiring a ghostwriter is an extravagant investment, however, rates can vary depending on the extent and complexity of the job, the writer's experience, and the client's budget. To satisfy clients' financial restraints, several ghostwriters provide flexible payment choices.

- Ghostwriters can read minds: Some people believe that ghostwriters have an incredible capacity to know exactly what their clients want without direct dialogue. In actuality, successful ghostwriting necessitates open and honest communication between the writer and the client to ensure that the final output meets the client's expectations.

- Ghostwriting is a simple method to make money: While ghostwriting can be a lucrative job for talented writers, it is not a simple way to make money. Ghostwriters must meet tight deadlines, conduct extensive research, and adapt to various writing styles while remaining anonymous.

- While ghostwriters may give some editing and proofreading services, their primary function is to create content from scratch based on the client's ideas and concepts. They are not only improving previous work but also creating new written stuff.

- While it is true that celebrities and public figures frequently hire ghostwriters for their books and public pronouncements, ghostwriting services are available to a wide spectrum of clientele. Working with ghostwriters may help entrepreneurs, business executives, subject matter experts, and even aspiring novelists bring their ideas to life.

- Ghostwriters lack a writing style: Some individuals believe that ghostwriters write in a generic, one-size-fits-all style. In actuality, professional ghostwriters can adjust their writing style to match the client's voice, tone, and preferences, resulting in a product that seems authentic to the client.

- Ghostwriters are simply freelancers: While many ghostwriters operate as independent contractors, some work for writing agencies or organizations that provide professional ghostwriting services. These agencies may have a staff of writers with varying experience to meet the needs of their clients.

- While non-fiction ghostwriting is common, ghostwriters can also work on fiction projects such as novels and short stories. They, like non-fiction projects, can help shape the plot, build characters, and provide a unified narrative.

- Ghostwriters are just English language experts: Ghostwriting necessitates more than just language skills. A skilled ghostwriter should have strong research abilities, an understanding of complex subjects, and the ability to capture the client's distinct voice and perspective.

- Despite the increased availability of writing tools and resources, ghostwriting thrives because it provides a specialized service tailored to the unique needs of clients who may lack the time, expertise, or writing skills to complete their projects effectively.

- Hiring a ghostwriter is a shortcut to publication success. The quality of the material, the topic's relevancy, and marketing efforts are all important aspects of successful publishing.

- While ghostwriters are hired to bring the client's vision to life, they are frequently involved in the creative process and may offer suggestions and ideas to improve the final result. Collaboration between the client and the ghostwriter is essential for producing a high-quality result.

Understanding the realities of ghostwriting helps to dispel these myths and emphasizes the value of the ghostwriter's role in assisting individuals and businesses in sharing their ideas and stories with the rest of the world.

Is it illegal to hire ghostwriters? Ghostwriting is not a crime. In truth, Calvin Coolidge was the last President of the United States. President who did not employ a full-time ghostwriter. Politicians, corporate leaders, and the publishing industry have all welcomed the practice.

PURPOSE OF GHOSTWRITING

There are many purposes for hiring ghostwriters...

There are numerous reasons why firms require ghostwriting. To begin with, not everyone has the time or the talent to create their material. Many business owners are too busy operating their businesses to sit down and generate content regularly. Hiring a ghostwriter enables them to delegate this duty and concentrate on other elements of their organization.

Second, ghostwriting enables businesses to benefit from the knowledge and experience of experienced writers. Ghostwriters have a vast understanding of a wide range of topics and industries, which they can apply to create compelling and helpful writing for organizations. This can assist organizations in producing high-quality content that is more likely to resonate with their target audience and achieve their objectives.

Third, ghostwriting can assist organizations in producing material more quickly and efficiently. Ghostwriters are professional writers who can research and compose material swiftly and efficiently on a tight deadline. This can save organizations time and allow them to post their material more rapidly, which is especially crucial for firms that need to stay up with the fast-paced world of Internet marketing.

Fourth, ghostwriting can assist firms in developing content that is specific to their intended audience. Ghostwriters can collaborate with businesses to better understand their target audience, goals, and preferences. This enables ghostwriters to create material that is carefully tailored to the target audience and achieve the intended effects.

In summary, ghostwriting is a great tool for businesses looking to create high-quality content without sacrificing time, resources, or brand voice. Businesses can have access to the skills and experience of professional writers by employing a professional ghostwriter, creating content faster and more efficiently, and personalizing their material to their intended audience. In today's competitive business world, ghostwriting can provide firms with the competitive advantage they require to flourish.

A SUCCESSFUL GHOSTWRITER'S SKILLS AND QUALITIES.

5 Skills a Ghostwriter Should Have

The following are some abilities that every ghostwriter should have:

1. **CONFIDENCE:** Confidence is essential to your success as a ghostwriter for a variety of reasons. Due to the fact that they can be engaged to write a book or a blog post, a self-assured ghostwriter is more likely to get clients. Your self-assurance can also make it easier to discuss tactics with your client to construct a piece of writing based on their thoughts.

Finally, knowing that you can write without a byline and that any accolades you receive for your work, whether an article or a book, may be directed at and received by your client will boost your confidence. If this thought makes you uncomfortable or resentful, try alternative types of writing careers.

2. **CREATIVITY**: A ghostwriter may be assigned to conceptualize and organize ideas, perform research, edit, and rewrite. As a freelance writer, you may have originated narrative ideas, organized articles or book chapters, and explored fresh approaches to previously published subjects. When ghostwriting, you can use the same talents.

3. **FLEXIBILITY:** Ghostwriters must be adaptable and versatile. You are responsible for conducting research and writing when you write your essay. When ghostwriting for a client, you may need to obtain information from that individual personally, whether in writing or via phone, email, or in-person conversations. Assume your client is unavailable when you require their assistance. In that instance, you can either extend the deadline or move on to another component of the project that does not require their immediate involvement. If you work to meet the client's deadlines, your client may not feel

required to complete the assignment on time, causing you to lag behind and possibly not get rewarded for your efforts. Your customer wants you to follow their instructions when you ghostwrite.

4. **Organizational skills**: This is less crucial if you're working on a quick assignment. Consider when you're ghostwriting a book. This requires you to organize the information you obtain from your customer, your research, many chapter modifications, and other relevant material. Manila folders can be used for book projects, and a Word folder can be used to arrange all of the research and chapters. Your methods may differ, but the main thing is to organize your resources, drafts, and correspondence in a way that works for you.

5. **Publishing knowledge**: This is less of an issue if you're ghostwriting shorter pieces like articles and blog posts, but if you want to ghostwrite novels for clients, you'll need to have some published works

beforehand. If you've had your books published by traditional publishers, you've received significant industry information that can help your clients. If you self-published using a print-on-demand or POD provider, your experience may be useful to clients who follow in your footsteps. Ghostwriters who have published formally and independently (in print, via e-books, or both) have a huge edge over authors who are outstanding writers but are unfamiliar with modern publishing.

"The more book experience you have, the more valuable you are to a customer and the more potential you have as a ghostwriter."

The Benefits and Drawbacks of Ghostwriting

The pros and cons of becoming a ghostwriter are summarized here.

Pros

➢ Ghostwriters might make money while working on their projects. Although you do not receive a byline, you are paid for your work. In the downtime between your ghostwriting assignments, you can work on your projects.

➤ Assignments can span practically any topic imaginable. You could be assigned to write about anything, whether it's a self-help book, the Vietnam War, or home design. If you enjoy doing research and are eager to learn about new topics, ghostwriting could be the job for you.

➤ You do not need any special qualifications to enter the field. A ghostwriter does not need advanced degrees or unique certificates. If you can write well, pay close attention to your author, and take careful notes, you can succeed as a ghostwriter.

"A successful ghostwriter is first and foremost an attentive listener, then a good writer."

➤ You are simply responsible for writing and nothing else. When the project is completed, your duties are also completed. You are not involved in the project's other components, such as production or marketing. Writers do not need to worry about making public appearances or conducting interviews to promote their books because it will be the author's responsibility.

➤ Ghostwriting can be lucrative once established in the field. Fast Company reports that less experienced ghostwriters can make $20,000 to $30,000 per assignment, while intermediate writers can earn more than $50,000. Early assignments, if established, can lead to larger and higher-paying ghostwriting gigs.

Cons

➤ Ghostwriting is a competitive industry. There are few such possibilities, and even fewer are freely publicized on job boards. Assignment leads can be difficult to locate, and developing contacts to find possible leads can be time-consuming. To find that first assignment, you must be patient and persistent.

➢ You must forego a byline. Your name is usually not printed on the finished product. You do all of the labor yet do not receive credit, but you are compensated.

➢ You must work for another person. You may or may not agree with the decisions that person takes. To work with them, you must set aside your ego, and you will have little control over the project's outcome.

➢ There could be tight deadlines and quick turnaround periods. Because the author wants to publish a book in response to current events, you may be expected to work longer hours to fulfill a deadline.

➢ The work may not be particularly intriguing. Even though ghostwriters may cover a wide range of topics, you may find them boring or beyond your area of expertise.

Consider the benefits and drawbacks of becoming a ghostwriter. Which of these circumstances are acceptable to you, and which are unacceptable?

It may be beneficial to speak with a few experienced ghostwriters to learn about their experiences. To learn more about this specialization, visit the Association of Ghostwriters.

Despite the drawbacks, ghostwriting for others can be a rewarding way to supplement your income while pursuing your interests.

WHAT EXACTLY IS CO-AUTHORING?

The practice of two or more people working together to generate a piece of scholarly or creative work, such as a research paper, journal article, book, or any other publication, is referred to as co-authorship.

Collaborative initiatives are widespread in academia and professional domains because they allow experts with diverse viewpoints and talents to contribute to a project. When two or more people collaborate on a piece of writing, they are referred to as co-authors.

Each co-author often contributes to the final product's development, research, writing, or editing. Their contributions can vary in magnitude, but each co-author is expected to contribute significantly intellectually or creatively to the work. Co-authorship is especially essential in academic research because it displays joint accountability for the work's content and findings.

The first author is usually the one who made the most substantial contribution, and the last author is usually the primary investigator or senior researcher who managed the study. To avoid disagreements or misunderstandings about the distribution of credit for the final publication, co-authors must communicate well, agree on the scope and direction of the effort, and define authorship criteria early on. Co-authorship processes are frequently governed by ethical norms and professional standards to provide fair and transparent recognition of each individual's contribution.

THE DISTINCTION BETWEEN CO-AUTHORING AND GHOSTWRITING:

Co-authorship and ghostwriting are two distinct writing and publishing processes with varying levels of involvement and acknowledgment for the individuals involved:

Co-authorship:

➤ As previously stated, co-authorship refers to the collaboration of two or more individuals who actively contribute to the creation of a piece of scholarly or creative work.

➢ Each co-author is thanked and credited for their contributions to the work. Their names are mentioned as authors, and they share responsibility for the publication's content and findings.

➢ Co-authors are required to contribute significantly intellectually or creatively to the project, such as research, writing, data analysis, or critical insights.

In contrast, when it comes to ghostwriting:

● In contrast, ghostwriting entails one person (the ghostwriter) creating content on behalf of another person or entity without obtaining clear credit or authorship.

● The ghostwriter's name is not included in the published work, and they remain uncredited.

● When individuals or organizations lack the time, experience, or writing skills to write material themselves, ghostwriting is frequently used. Ghostwriters are often hired to create books, articles, speeches, or other materials, and the work is credited to the person or entity who hired them. The person who claims credit for the ghostwritten work is typically referred to as the "author" or "named author," even though they did not physically write the content.

The primary distinction between co-authorship and ghostwriting is the degree of credit and acknowledgment. Co-authors actively participate in the creation of the work and are properly credited, whereas ghostwriters remain nameless and are not publicly recognized for their contributions. Both activities are legal when carried out ethically and transparently, as long as all parties responsibilities and contributions are properly revealed.

Here are a few more things to think about when it comes to co-authorship and ghostwriting:

Co-authorship:

- Collaboration: The emphasis of co-authorship is on collaboration and teamwork. It enables people with a wide range of experience to pool their knowledge and abilities to produce high-quality work.
- Academic Integrity: Accurate co-authorship attribution is critical for maintaining academic integrity in academic and research environments. To avoid plagiarism and secure proper credit, researchers must follow the ethical norms established by academic institutions and publishers.
- Author Order: The order in which co-authors are mentioned can be significant. The first author is frequently the key contributor, with succeeding authors contributing in descending order of importance. The last author is usually the project's senior researcher or main investigator.

GHOSTWRITING:

- Anonymity: Ghostwriters prefer to remain nameless or refuse to accept credit for their work. Their contributions are largely "invisible" to the general population.
- Professional Service: Ghostwriting is a competent writer's professional service. It enables individuals, public figures, or organizations to publish information under their names without having to spend the time or effort writing it themselves.
- Ethical difficulties: Ghostwriting can pose ethical difficulties, especially when public figures or experts promote the work as completely their own without admitting the ghostwriter's contribution.
- Confidentiality: Ghostwriters frequently work under contracts or agreements that ensure their

involvement is kept private. This secrecy is essential for maintaining the illusion that the "named author" is the lone creator of the work.

- Legal Agreements: In some circumstances, ghostwriting relationships are formalized through legal agreements entered into between the ghostwriter and the person or entity receiving credit for the work. These agreements spell out the project's terms, as well as payment and confidentiality obligations. It is critical to understand that when done ethically and transparently, both co-authorship and ghostwriting can be beneficial and acceptable procedures. Clear communication, correct attribution, and adherence to ethical principles are critical in academic and professional settings to promote fairness and integrity in publishing and creative pursuits.

YOU SHOULD KNOW THESE FAMOUS GHOSTWRITERS

Here are seven well-known ghostwriters:

✓ Andrew Neiderman is the ghostwriter for the "V.C. Andrews' "Flowers in the Attic" is part of this series.

✓ Ian Fleming (with later authors) - Created James Bond and penned multiple Bond novels, but after his death, the series was continued by other writers such as Kingsley Amis and Anthony Horowitz.

✓ Andrew Crofts is a well-known ghostwriter who has contributed to several celebrity memoirs and biographies.

✓ Known for developing the "Jason Bourne" series, Robert Ludlum (with additional authors) kept publishing books in the series after his death.

✓ H.P. Lovecraft (to a degree) - While not solely a ghostwriter, Lovecraft frequently ghostwrote or altered works for other authors.

✓ Rosie Knightley is a well-known ghostwriter who specializes in romance and women's fiction works.

✓ William Novak - A ghostwriter who has worked on famous memoirs like Magic Johnson and Lee Iacocca.

These ghostwriters have helped shape a variety of creative works, allowing authors to keep their anonymity or work on many projects at the same time.

CHAPTER 2

THE LIFE OF A GHOSTWRITER

Just why ghostwrite? I have attempted self-publishing. The process of marketing and selling your books takes time. It's simpler, less stressful, requires less promotion, and pays handsomely to ghostwrite. So, a few years ago, I conducted some study on ghostwriting before learning via a blog post. My $1 per page rate was a significant undercharge, according to the analysis.

I received barely $70 for the first eBook I ever ghostwrote, which was almost 70 pages long. I will charge between $1 and $2 per word in 2023. For creative work like fiction, I charge more than for nonfiction. The rate rises if the task requires considerable study.

This indicates that I could easily make $10,000 by ghostwriting a 10,000-word novella. Imagine the remuneration for a 60,000–100,000 word book now. Many authors are unaware of the profitable niche of ghostwriting.

Do You Want to Be a Ghostwriter?

If you take great pride in your writing, ghostwriting is probably not for you. It can, however, be your area of expertise if you want to manipulate the ideas of others and turn them into your own.

Is the pay for ghostwriting higher than for traditional writing?

Yes, it does, but wealth doesn't come to you instantly. Some independent ghostwriters say they earn six figures annually. They do make that much money, but not straight soon.

IMPROVE YOUR WRITING SKILLS

In today's information-driven society, improving writing abilities via instruction, practice, and ongoing learning is crucial. Effective written communication is an essential ability that applies to many facets of life, including academic, professional, and personal. Writing effectively not only facilitates the straightforward communication of ideas but also improves the ability to think critically, be creative, and solve problems. To satisfy the various requirements of customers and projects, aspirant ghostwriters in particular need to concentrate on strengthening their writing skills.

A writer's abilities are fundamentally shaped by their education. Grammar, vocabulary, and compositional conventions are all well-established thanks to formal schooling. It helps prospective authors get familiar with numerous writing genres and styles so they can appreciate the subtle differences between them.

Studying creative writing, literature, or journalism may provide authors with the skills they need to create gripping stories and successfully engage readers. But education on its own is insufficient. Regular practice is necessary to become proficient at writing. Writing becomes better with practice just like any other ability. Aspiring ghostwriters should schedule time each day to write, experimenting with various genres and topics.

Regular writing aids in skill development, voice discovery, and confidence building. To get feedback and learn from others, they may run their blogs, take part in writing contests, or post content in online writing groups.

For authors to stay current and adaptive in a changing market, continuous learning is essential.

The publishing industry is constantly changing due to shifting trends and client preferences. Particularly for ghostwriting, it's important to be adaptable and able to change your writing style to fit the needs of different clients and projects. A writer's abilities may be greatly improved by reading extensively across genres and keeping up with the most recent writing tools and practices.

Aspiring ghostwriters might concentrate on the following areas for development to match the needs of diverse projects:

❖ Ghostwriters often work on a variety of themes with which they may be unfamiliar. Strong research abilities enable them to compile reliable data and provide well-informed material.

❖ Collaborative Skills: Working closely with clients or editors is a common task for ghostwriters. Writers should be open to modifications, attentive to criticism, and skilled at anticipating and exceeding clients' needs.

- ❖ Versatility: Writing for a variety of material types, including books, blogs, essays, and site copy, opens up more chances for ghostwriters.

- ❖ Time management: In the writing profession, meeting deadlines is essential. To produce high-quality work within the allotted period, ghostwriters must learn to manage their time effectively.

- ❖ Editing and proofreading: Developing self-editing abilities guarantees that the final products are polished and error-free, which minimizes the need for significant revisions.

- ❖ Building a Portfolio: To show prospective customers, aspiring ghostwriters should compile a portfolio of their greatest work. This may include both compensated and unpaid work, showcasing their versatility and talent.

- ❖ Reading as a Foundation: Reading often is a key component in improving writing abilities. Reading works in a variety of genres and styles exposes authors to diverse writing processes, aids in vocabulary growth, and inspires original writing.

❖ Seeking Mentorship: Up-and-coming ghostwriters might gain a lot by working with more seasoned authors or editors as mentors. A mentor may provide insightful advice, supportive counsel, and helpful criticism to accelerate the development of writing skills.

❖ Understanding the Target Audience: Writers, particularly ghostwriters, need to be aware of who their projects' target audiences are. The text will successfully connect with the reader if the writing style and tone are adjusted to their preferences.

❖ Learning from Feedback: Getting feedback, whether it comes from colleagues, customers, or editors, is a chance for improvement. Writers may improve their skills by accepting constructive criticism and adopting ideas into the next works.

❖ Experimenting with Different Voices: Since ghostwriters often have to write from the viewpoint of others, they frequently need to use several voices and tones. Writing in a variety of voices helps writers become more adaptable and versatile.

❖ Accepting the Writing Process: The process of writing is seldom linear. The writing process, which involves brainstorming, outlining, drafting, rewriting, and editing, should be embraced by aspiring ghostwriters. Each step is essential to creating material of the highest quality.

❖ Staying Ethical: When working on assignments, ghostwriters must uphold moral standards and observe confidentiality. They should be careful to provide their client with unique content and prevent plagiarism.

❖ Building a network within the literary community may lead to new possibilities and collaborations, thus networking and developing relationships are important.

❖ Making contacts with other authors, editors, and future customers may be very beneficial.

❖ Keeping Up with Industry Trends: Just like any other industry, writing develops with time. Ghostwriters may adapt and maintain their competitiveness by being knowledgeable about the most recent developments, publication platforms, and marketing techniques. Writing regularly is important for progress, but aspirant ghostwriters should also concentrate on maintaining the quality of their work. Maintaining a balance between output and quality guarantees your continuing development as a writer.

Developing writing abilities via instruction, practice, and ongoing learning is crucial for all authors, but it's especially important for aspiring ghostwriters.

By investing in their writing skills, they may successfully handle the demands of various projects, establish a solid name in the field, and open the door for a fruitful and satisfying writing career. Writing is a path of development and self-discovery, and those who are dedicated to becoming better will find that they are consistently becoming proficient and in-demand experts.

TRAVELING IN THE WORLD OF PUBLICATION

The following are some obstacles and difficulties that prospective ghostwriters could run against while trying to establish themselves as respectable experts:

❖ Lack of Portfolio and Experience: The lack of a strong portfolio is one of the major challenges for beginners. Clients often seek ghostwriters with a track record and professional expertise. Without a portfolio displaying their writing talents, aspiring ghostwriters can find it difficult to get customers.

❖ Building Credibility and Trust: A high degree of trust between the writer and the customer is necessary for ghostwriting. When clients entrust ghostwriters with their private material, they often demand expertise and discretion in return. For individuals who are just starting, it may be challenging to establish a reputation as a dependable and trustworthy ghostwriter.

❖ Finding customers: Since the ghostwriting business mainly depends on word-of-mouth recommendations and existing contacts, finding early customers may be challenging. Identifying and connecting with prospective customers who need their services might be difficult for aspiring ghostwriters.

❖ Negotiating prices: For beginners, determining reasonable and competitive prices may be challenging. Particularly if the writer lacks expertise or confidence in how to price their services, some customers may attempt to bargain for cheaper fees or undervalue the work of ghostwriters.

❖ Ghostwriters must be flexible and able to write in a variety of tones and styles to satisfy the preferences of their customers. This adaptability may be difficult, particularly for authors who are more at ease with a certain writing style.

❖ Ghostwriters often work on sensitive projects that need signing non-disclosure agreements (NDAs). Some wannabe ghostwriters may be concerned about the obligations and potential legal repercussions associated with handling private material.

❖ Lack of Recognition: In contrast to conventional authors, ghostwriters seldom ever get credit for their work in the media. For authors hoping to gain recognition and exposure in the literary community, this obscurity may be demoralizing. Balancing Personal Writing Objectives: Many prospective ghostwriters have personal writing goals and projects. It might be challenging to strike a balance between pursuing personal writing ambitions and working as a ghostwriter for customers.

Advice for Future Ghostwriters:
Build a Portfolio: To demonstrate your abilities and adaptability, start by compiling a portfolio of writing examples. To show prospective customers your expertise, you may publish articles, blog posts, or short tales.

- Attend writing conferences, seminars, and online forums to network and engage with other authors and business leaders. Networking might result in recommendations and new possibilities.

- Offer Freelance skills: To get experience and establish a name for yourself in the writing community, start by offering your skills as a freelance writer.

- Improve Versatility: Write in many genres and styles to increase your adaptability as a ghostwriter. Clients often look for authors who can effectively convey their voices.

- To negotiate a reasonable price for your job, research the market rates and industry norms for ghostwriting costs.

- Sign NDAs with Care: If you have any questions before signing an NDA, see a lawyer to help you understand your rights and obligations.

- Be Patient and Persistent: It takes time and perseverance to get into the ghostwriting business. Continue improving your abilities and applying to positions that fit them. Always keep in mind that building a reputation and success as a ghostwriter takes time, hard effort, professionalism, and regularly providing customers with high-quality work. Aspiring ghostwriters may succeed in this distinctive and lucrative sector if they overcome these obstacles with tenacity and dedication to developing a solid reputation.

EARLY EXPERIENCES AND FIRST PROJECT

There are many chances for budding ghostwriters to develop their skills and portfolios via early tasks. These assignments might be modest employment or partnerships with less well-known writers. Here are a few examples of early experiences that may serve as inspiration for you: The Blogging Sidekick: In the beginning, an aspirant ghostwriter called Alex acquired a modest job assisting a travel blogger in keeping up a regular posting schedule. Despite having brilliant thoughts, the blogger had trouble successfully expressing them in words. Alex put a lot of effort into writing interesting posts about far-off places and travel advice to realize the blogger's aim.

With the help of this project, Alex improved their writing abilities and mastered the talent of changing their voice to fit the blogger's style. The success of this partnership created other possibilities to collaborate with other bloggers, laying the groundwork for a successful ghostwriting career. Ella, an aspiring author with a love for fiction, made a connection with a less well-known author who had great tale ideas but lacked the time and self-assurance to transform them into full-length books. Ella gladly gave her assistance, working closely with the author to comprehend the concepts, characters, and storylines they had in mind. They collaborated to write engrossing books that were well-received by both readers and reviewers. Ella could polish her narrative skills as a result of the experience, which also helped the author gain exposure and land additional book sales and collaboration chances.

The Celebrity Speechwriter: By chance, James, a budding ghostwriter with experience in speech and debate, received a recommendation to assist a less well-known public person with their speeches. Despite not being well-known, the person spoke at several events and required compelling material to connect with the audience. James worked hard to construct speeches that connected with the speaker's unique experiences and convictions. A developing reputation as a proficient speechwriter and invitations to additional high-profile events resulted from the relationship. Thanks to the expertise obtained from working with a less well-known public person, James finally got a job with a well-known celebrity.

The Niche Expert:

Samantha, an aspiring ghostwriter who is passionate about nutrition and wellbeing, chose to work with an unheralded health celebrity. The influencer wanted to increase their audience by releasing an ebook on healthy living since they had a dedicated but tiny following. Samantha happily accepted the task, doing extensive research on the most recent health trends and writing the book's content with skill. The booklet received favorable reviews and soon gained popularity, bringing Samantha and the health influencer a flood of new customers. Through this early partnership, Samantha not only confirmed her standing as an authority in the wellness sector but also as a dependable ghostwriter for professionals across a range of businesses.

The ambitious ghostwriters in each of these tales pounced on chances to collaborate with less well-known individuals and used these endeavors as stepping stones to larger successes. They developed their careers and acquired priceless experiences that pushed them toward more big undertakings in the future by showcasing their abilities, commitment, and capacity to bring someone else's vision to reality. Remember that any chance, no matter how tiny, might be a stepping stone to success as you begin your ghostwriting adventure. Accept the difficulties, gain knowledge from each assignment, and use your imagination to transform even the most basic concepts into engrossing literary masterpieces.

CHAPTER 3

COLLABORATING WITH CLIENTS

Interview Techniques for Ghostwritters

Without some form of interviewing procedure, book ghostwriting CANNOT succeed. How are you ever going to provide a final product that embodies the client's voice and vision if you don't call them and talk about the book's structure, objectives, and content? You aren't. Period. However, not everyone learns interviewing techniques in class or daily life. Even someone like myself who has taken journalism classes finds it scary. Most authors are reclusive introverts who prefer to spend their time alone with a book rather than socialize with others. Phone talks are even more daunting since you can't see the other person's face. It's easy to speak for an hour at an interview if you're not acquainted with the procedure, even when you get the guts to do so (since, after all, this is your chosen career; what else are you going to do?).

But don't worry; I've got a few tips up my sleeve for making interviews a bit less daunting and a lot more fruitful owing to my minor in communications.

Putting the Client at Ease and You

Before accepting the assignment, you probably previously had a conversation with this customer about it. If you didn't, you should establish that as a routine. If you don't do some kind of preliminary interview (over the phone or by email), you can't provide an accurate estimate, fair to the customer, and appropriately compensates you for all the labor required.

In the first interview after the contracts have been signed and the first payment made, warm up the professional rapport you've previously built. Getting the customer to speak about themselves is the greatest method to do this. Do not inquire about your children's names or other personal information. That is spooky. The following are examples of such questions: "What inspired you to create this book? "Why do you adore [insert the book's subject]? This maintains things professional while also demonstrating interest in the customers' hobbies and encouraging them to talk openly about their passions.

Additionally, you might make general inquiries such as, "Where are you from?"How are things today? The trick here is to engage in light chat to ease both of your anxiety. These kinds of common queries help individuals feel more at case. By the time you reach that point, you will have greatly warmed up the customer to you and hardly have to speak.

ASKING THE RIGHT QUESTIONS

When it comes to business, the inquiries must be more focused. Always, always, always enter a client interview prepared and with thoughtful questions. I usually try to get at least 10, at least at first. Get as many good questions as you can at first; as you grow more acquainted with the project, your inquiries will become even more focused and you won't need as many.

So, where do you get the ideas for such questions?

1) You ought to be aware of the book's intended readership and the client's overarching editorial goals. Now consider the audience's expectations for a book of this kind. Make careful to address the audience when you pose such queries.

2) Do you still have any unresolved questions about the client's vision for this book? Do you still need

further information about the client's objectives for the project? Pose those inquiries.

3) You have the overall picture in mind (or you should, based on preliminary interviews), but you need to organize this book such that the reader has a seamless and engaging experience. Ask your customer what he or she thinks of your ideas after coming up with a couple of ways to accomplish them. Which one does the customer favor? Does the customer have any other structural suggestions?

4) Consider the material itself. What is the project's scope? What research has already been conducted and what needs to be compiled? Do you personally have any queries to aid in your comprehension of the subject?

Once you've addressed the most important issues, you can begin writing. As you write, you'll likely uncover additional queries you anticipate readers having, structural flaws, or information your client wants to add. There is no general advice I can provide you since they will be quite content-specific. My recommendation is to ask the customer questions, regardless of how personal they may be, or if you're worried you'll come out as being uninformed about the subject. If a person employs a ghost, they must be prepared to get a bit personal, or they won't discover that they are the subject of their book. And it's far preferable to provide little or inaccurate information than to ask a "dumb" inquiry. Aside from making your customers feel like an authority on the subject, doing so ensures that you include their opinions and knowledge in the book.

I begin by asking the big questions about the book as a whole, then I have an interview before writing each chapter where we discuss the content, and finally, after I have a rough draft of that chapter read, I hold another call to get those small details that tie it all together before delivering the chapter for review.

When Issues Become Personal

Any factual work is made more engaging by personal tales. In fiction, everything is a tale, but in nonfiction, you'll want to find methods to make the material your own and keep readers interested. Anecdotes are the best tool for doing this. The whole memoir is a personal tale if you're writing one.

Such queries might be challenging to ask. Sometimes the topic matter is delicate, and other times your customer isn't giving you anything to work with since they can't remember or aren't prodding them well enough. So how can you get customers to share personal experiences?

Always Ask Open-Ended Questions: You need to encourage a customer to speak freely if you want to get a lot of information from them rather than just a yes or no response. The easiest approach to do this is to formulate your inquiries in a manner that precludes a yes-or-no response. Rather than posing the query, "Did it make you angry? pose a question like, "What was your first gut response when you received that first rejection? How were you feeling? How did you act? However, you also don't want to be overly generic, since customers often want some guidance. Instead of asking, "What occurred next? You may try asking, "What did you decide to do about it? " or "How did you get from being rejected to where you are now?"

If your client is being reticent to speak, try rephrasing the same inquiry in several ways to get them to start talking. The more times your customer hears that question or a version of it, the more used he or she grows to it and the more time they have to come up with a response. "How did that make you feel when she said that? " eliciting no reaction. Try, "Did her statements make you angry, sad, or confused? If you merely get a brief, impersonal response like "sad," you might follow up by asking "Why? Try rephrasing it once again with, "So, it upset you a good deal, understandably. " If that still doesn't inspire you to create a scenario. How did you feel when she said it? Have you yelled at her? cried you? Or did you remain quiet? Giving your customers alternatives like this, in my experience, causes their memories to become more vivid because their minds will tell them, "No, it didn't go that way... sure, sure, I did that, and then this occurred,

Dealing with Clients Who Talk Too Much

This is not at all a terrible thing. It is preferable to the next kind of customer that we will discuss. However, issues still arise from it. Your customer may not be too pleased with that cost if you charge by the hour for your interviews (I don't; I just incorporate that time into my per-word or fixed fee rate). You certainly don't want this to happen if you're not.

Why? Well, a chatty customer is only beneficial if they are conversing about the appropriate topics. You won't succeed if your customer spends the first 10 minutes of the interview gushing about the fantastic new restaurant he just had lunch at.

Developing your corralling skills is essential if you want to deal with people who speak too much. You need to overcome your social anxiety and stop the customer if they start talking about anything irrelevant. Say the client's name to draw them in, followed by a question like, "Could you tell me a bit more about _____? or "Could you clarify _____ a little more? You'll notice that in each of those situations, you explain why you need to cover this issue rather than what they were rambling on about. I believe we need a few more clear examples so we don't lose any of the readers.

I can assure you that if you offer excessively chatty customers something else to speak about, they won't take offense at the interruption and, if you simply take the initiative to steer them in the proper path, they'll have no issue giving you what you need to know.

The management of reserved clients

The real doozy is this. These are the customers who are reticent, who tend to withdraw owing to sensitive emotions, or who are so knowledgeable about their subject that they don't feel the need to go into great depth. These are the customers you have to force answers from, much as you would force gum off your foot or push open an old, rusty steel door with a crowbar.

Fortunately, I haven't encountered any while working on tasks for my communications courses, but I have certainly come across a couple of them.

First, if you're working with one, be sure you've taken all reasonable steps to establish a rapport with the customer. Before beginning the actual task, have a short conversation to establish some common ground. speak a bit about yourself if they are reluctant to speak about themselves. Demonstrate your faith in them. This may make a hesitant customer feel at ease if you're working with them.

Use the rephrasing strategy I discussed in the "When Things Get Personal" section if the client is becoming reticent because the topic is personal. Additionally, if the circumstance is very difficult—such as the death of a loved one, a childhood abuse history, or a drug addiction—take time to say something like, "I realize this is difficult, but you wanted to get this out there to assist others in similar circumstances, right? This narrative, in my opinion, is quite significant, and I believe many of your readers will identify with it. We can take a break if you get too uncomfortable, but let's give it a go first, okay?"

You should prepare a big list of questions for the interview in case the expert you're speaking with thinks their knowledge is obvious and isn't providing you with enough details. You still need to have a thorough understanding of the subject even if the book is intended for other experts rather than novices. If you've taken on a job like that, you presumably have some knowledge of the subject, so put up a list of intelligent inquiries that will provide you with all the information you need to write that book convincingly. That expert should have no trouble responding to your specific queries as long as they can see you've done your research and merely need some clarity.

If you find out you're working with a novice on the subject who just wanted to write this book to earn some money, I'm sorry, but you're in a terrible position. No matter how you ask the question, the customer won't be able to aid you; the only option is to transition from routine interviews to extensive research. I'm hoping you charged appropriately. Another justification for the need for first interviews.

Final Reflections

Interviews aren't as terrifying as your stomach's churning or the annoying voice in your brain makes them out to be. Even though I still feel nervous the first time I meet a new client, I've discovered that as long as I have my questions ready, I can quickly become comfortable. You are in command of the interview if you have any questions. All anxieties disappear after the first interviews. Ghostwriting customers rapidly become friends since you discuss ideas with them, swap personal stories, and collaborate on projects as a group throughout the process. It's hard to avoid developing some type of connection.

To feel comfortable and in control throughout the interview process, use these suggestions to get past any stumbling blocks and create your strategies depending on your clients and preferences.

The Collaborative Process: Ghostwriters and Authors Come Together

● Increasing communication and trust establishes a solid working connection by being open and honest with one another. Recognizing the author's intentions, objectives, and project expectations.

● Charting the Course Outlining the structure, major themes, and character arcs of the novel collectively. discussing the main ideas, takeaways, and objectives to match the author's goals with the ghostwriter's experience.

- Feedback loops are repeated often to make sure the ghostwriter is capturing the author's objectives. incorporating changes and modifying depending on the author's suggestions.

Five ways to improve client communication, including its components

Establishing trust with customers and clearly articulating requirements, expectations, and any obstacles are made possible through effective communication. Effective communication may enhance customer relationships and even generate more leads for the company.

What exactly is customer communication?

Client communication is any exchange of information between a business and its clients. This may involve verbal and written communication (such as emails and bills), as well as physical communication (such as smiling). Active listening is a key component of effective client communication since it helps you understand your client's feelings and better meet their requirements.

Why is it crucial to communicate with clients?

Because it builds and preserves trust between the customer and the company, contact with the client is crucial. Customers may be more inclined to stick with a company if they feel confident in it. Open lines of contact with customers may also reduce misunderstandings, increase client happiness, and increase consumer referrals.

Five Components of Effective Client

Communication Companies with excellent, transparent communication may build stronger bonds with their customers.

Here are the key components of effective customer communication:

- **The openness**

Being open and honest with a customer promotes trust. Customers could value knowing more about the manufacturing process so they can make informed purchasing decisions and support organizations they value. Customers may feel more at ease making purchases if they comprehend how your company runs and what its bottom line is.

Being open and honest with customers' requirements and with any price or policy changes or other company developments that may have an impact on them are further examples of transparency.

- **Be flexible**

Having flexible communication options may improve the connection between the customer and the company. Flexibility enables both sides to maintain communication when a change happens. For instance, flexibility enables a company to maintain communication with customers if its phone lines go down by putting up online chat rooms or conference calls.

Businesses may demonstrate flexibility by offering accessible communication channels. For instance, employing a specialized translator may demonstrate to customers that a company values its business and cares about preserving positive connections when a sizable section of the customer base speaks a language other than the company's principal working language.

● **Compassion and empathy**
Employees with these interpersonal abilities better understand customers and companies. The act of feeling sympathy for someone who is in need is known as compassion. Understanding another person's viewpoint is the act of having empathy.

By picturing the emotions a client could feel amid change or an unexpected requirement, you might develop empathy for them. Businesses may engage with customers more personally by using these talents.

- **Self-awareness**

Companies that excel in communication also exercise self-awareness. This entails analyzing its goods, services, and brand image to find possibilities for development.
Self-awareness also enables a company to acknowledge its flaws and discover its strengths. You may increase customer trust by admitting mistakes and demonstrating to them how you're fixing them.

Advice for enhancing customer interaction:
Here are some suggestions to help you communicate with your customers more effectively:

• Facilitate communication

Customers value businesses that make it simple to contact them. For instance, having your company's contact information accessible makes communication simpler. Consider making yourself more accessible to communication by including contact details on your website and social media profiles. Email addresses, customer service phone lines, and comment sections are examples of this. Making communication easy for customers communicates your want to hear from them.

Maintaining respect is essential to building a trustworthy connection. Communication is also important. Clients are more inclined to appreciate you when you treat them with respect. Respecting limits is another aspect of maintaining respect.

Expect and thank others for their input, since it is essential for polite, open discussion to take place. Feedback from clients may be a fantastic method to understand their expectations and correct any misunderstandings.

Quality feedback gives a company the chance to assess its strengths and flaws by looking at itself from the client's viewpoint. On your website, social media accounts, or receipts, you may solicit feedback. Encourage customers to provide in-depth feedback to get the desired outcomes.

A SAMPLE EMAIL THANKING OTHERS FOR THEIR COMMENTS

(Hi Peter,

I wanted to personally thank you for the feedback you gave our team earlier this week. I had noticed some inefficiencies early in the life of our project but was unable to identify the processes that were causing them. Your comments have given so much clarity to the mistakes we made throughout our project, and I am now motivated to move forward with your feedback in mind as I approach my next project.

Best,

Godwin)

The Best Ghostwriting Advice for Getting Your Client's Voice Through

Recognizing Your Client

Conduct in-depth interviews: Spend time getting to know your customer before you begin writing. Conduct in-depth interviews to learn about their history, experiences, beliefs, and objectives. Look closely at their personality, tastes, and peculiarities. You'll be more able to write in your customer's voice the more you comprehend your client.

Read any previously published material from your client, such as blog entries, articles, or speeches. Pay attention to their narrative methods, language, sentence structure, and tone. This will provide you with important insights into their writing style and make it easier for you to imitate it.

Listen and observe: Focus on your client's communication style in casual chats in addition to interviews and written work. Pay attention to their word choices, speaking patterns, and voice cadence. Pay attention to their behaviors, gestures, and body language. These details will give your work depth and authenticity.

Developing Your Voice.

Develop Empathy: The foundation of ghostwriting is empathy. Consider yourself your customers, and try to comprehend them from their point of view. Consider their feelings, aspirations, and challenges. You'll be able to record your client's voice more accurately if you can relate to them on an emotional level.

Start with a Writing Sample: Request a writing sample from your customer or ask them to draft a brief essay on a pertinent subject. You may use this as a point of reference to comprehend their writing voice and style. To emulate their style and wording in your ghostwriting, use this example as a starting point.

Use Appropriate Language and Tone: Pay special attention to the language and tone your customer often employs. Write to reflect any industrial jargon or professional terminology that they often employ. Likewise, if their style is more informal and conversational, adjust. The writing will seem natural and true to the voice of your customer if terminology and tone are consistent.

Writing Strategies for Developing Voice.

Listen to Audio Recordings: To hear your client's voice in its most natural state, record their conversations or speeches if at all feasible. To learn the intonations, rhythms, and speech patterns of the people in these recordings, listen to them frequently. This will make it easier for you to write in their distinct voice.

Incorporate Dialogue and Anecdotes: Include dialogue and anecdotes that are based on actual discussions and experiences your customer has had. This gives it a more personal touch and makes it easier for readers to relate to the author. When employing conversation, try to imitate the client's mannerisms and speaking patterns.

Mimic Sentence Form: Take note of the format and length of your client's sentences. Do they like short, punchy phrases or do they prefer longer, more detailed ones? Their sentence structure makes a huge contribution to their unique voice, therefore adapt your writing to reflect it.

Edit with Care: After finishing the first draft, carefully go over and edit your work to make sure it reflects your client's voice. Eliminate any words or phrases that don't seem like they fit their style. Maintaining their voice while making sure the information is polished and coherent must be balanced carefully.

Collaboration and Communication

Request Feedback: Keep in regular contact with your customer while the writing is being done. Share drafts or excerpts to get comments and make required changes. By working together, you can be confident that you're adhering to their goal and get their advice as required.

Open Lines of Contact: Establish open lines of contact with your customer that are transparent. Invite them to express their ideas, opinions, and worries. The more you talk to them, the easier it will be to adjust your writing to reflect their voice.

Increasing Your Toolkit for Ghostwriting

- Create a Style Guide for Your Client: A Style Guide for Your Client will help you consistently capture their voice. Include instructions regarding tone, vocabulary, preferred grammar, and formatting. This document acts as a starting point and guarantees that the client's distinctive voice and writing style will be preserved in all subsequent work.

- Have Regular Check-ins With Your Client: As a ghostwriter, it's important to often check in with your client to go through current projects, get feedback, and handle any issues. In addition to fostering a deeper working connection, these check-ins provide chances for you to match your writing to any updates or changes in the client's voice and message.

- Conduct Extensive Research: You may need to do in-depth research on your client's business, target market, or certain themes they want to address to effectively convey their voice. By doing research, you may learn more about their subject matter and write authoritatively and proficiently while accurately capturing their voice.

Upholding Integrity and Confidentiality

Sign nondisclosure agreements: When ghostwriting, sensitive or secret material is often involved. Non-disclosure agreements (NDAs) are necessary to safeguard your client's privacy. These contracts make sure you don't divulge any information, claim authorship of the material you generate, or violate confidentiality.

Deliver precisely and on time: Ghostwriting assignments often have due dates. It is essential to constantly achieve these deadlines and provide high-quality work. Pay close attention to the little things, proofread thoroughly, and make sure your work is flawless. You establish confidence and trust with your customers by being professional and completing assignments on schedule.

CHAPTER 4

ETHICS AND CONFIDENTIALITY IN GHOSTWRITING

Ghostwriting is a well-known notion in today's digital environment. Many Indians work as ghostwriters all around the world, even though Western nations have a larger industrial presence. Even powerful individuals give their services to someone else as a ghostwriter.

'Vikram and Betal' is a well-known Indian folktale. According to legend, Betal, a ghost, struck a deal with Vikram, the King, promising to accompany him as long as the latter listens to his tales and stays silent; if not, Betal will return. Similar to when a ghostwriter is engaged, he must act as the silent ruler and represent the genuine author. The agreement is broken if he opens his lips, i.e. uses his name, in contravention of the clause. Although this relationship works very well in reality, it seems unfair and unlawful when seen through the prism of intellectual property rights. It also prompts a lot of queries.

Ghostwriting

Ghostwriter is a term that requires little explanation. Any wise man may understand that the phrase refers to a writer who writes but gives credit to someone else. An author enters into a written agreement with independent writers to provide material for them in exchange for a predetermined payment. The recruiting procedure for a ghostwriter is described by Debora Weber-Wulff as follows: First, an assistant prepares some content. Then, before publication, something is written by a research assistant and revised by the researcher. When a document is then approved without alteration under the pressure to publish more and more, the real author is kept a secret, and the researcher does not even notice anything is wrong with this.

The employer is given full credit, and the worker gets compensated for any original effort. The authors often pay upfront or in installments. The work cannot be attributed to the ghostwriter in any way. There is a ton of stuff online nowadays thanks huge thousands and thousands of ghostwriters working all over the globe. It is a fantastic chance to get some extra revenue. For those whose primary occupation is writing, ghostwriting is a full-time career. Some of them either operate as independent contractors or join a ghostwriting business or partnership.

The practice of ghostwriting extends beyond online publications. In many cases, paid spirits write books and novels. Unbeknownst to many, it is a typical occurrence for prominent authors to have ideas for books but not enough time to make them a reality.

As a result, they employ a writer to act as their ghost to work their magic and transform the concept into actual work.

As the idea of contractual terms is implied, there may be various conditions for various kinds of employment. The ghostwriter may also be granted certain rights or financial compensation from the author. They may be employed on a temporary or permanent basis, and they may be paid upfront or in installments, depending on the job.

Copyright

A creator's copyright is a kind of intellectual property right. Original works are protected by copyright. The Indian Copyright Act, Section 14, defines copyright as an exclusive right, subject to its restrictions, to perform or authorize the performance of any of the aforementioned actions about a work or any significant portion of it. It contains pieces like these:

- A piece of literature, theater, or music that is not a computer program.
- Computer program
- Creative work
- Film for cinematography
- Sound capture

Ghostwriting and copyrighting

Section 2(o) of the Act defines the literary work referred to in Section 14 of the Act. A computer program, tables, and compilations, including a computer database, are all considered literary works by the aforementioned Section. The author of a literary work is the exclusive owner of the copyright to that work. The Copyright Act's defining clause also mentions computer-generated works. A computer-generated work's author is defined as the person who developed the work under Section 2(d) clause (g). The World Trade Organization's TRIPS Agreement establishes extensive guidelines for intellectual property rights, including copyright, on a global scale. Countries then implement these standards by their preferences and domestic laws.

The initial author, the employer, often enjoys the copyright in circumstances of employment or contracts of service. By Indian law, Section 17(a) states that the proprietor shall be the first owner of the work insofar as the copyright relates to the publication of the work when the work is created by an employee while they are employed or performing services under a contract of service or an apprenticeship. The paragraph goes on to say that the author will be the original proprietor of all other works. In contrast to the US, the work-for-hire theory is implemented under Section 17. In India, the individual who commissions a piece may also become its first owner, but they cannot also be considered the "first author."

When writers and authors in India opt to utilize their intelligence for someone else, the law itself restricts their rights, even though they previously enjoyed unrestricted control over their works. By loosening the provisions of the service contract, the rights are further made mobile. Therefore, if a ghostwriter chooses to operate independently, they have extensive and complete control over their output. If they can bargain, they may also assert their rights. It is difficult for a ghostwriter to negotiate a fair agreement because of the abundance of content writers both online and offline. Furthermore, it won't be ghostwriting if the paid writer receives the proper credit. It'll turn into co-authorship.

Copywriting

Another word used in the literary sector is copywriting. It is the procedure through which material for marketing and advertising is created. Copy is the term for the written material produced to raise brand recognition. A clone of this is also made to advertise the genuine product.

The main differences between ghostwriting and copywriting are as follows:

- The creator of the piece does not have to remain anonymous in copywriting. He may take credit for his creations. If one is a ghostwriter, then this is impossible.

- Furthermore, copywriting creates text only for the goal of advertising, unlike ghostwriting, whose purposes might range from literature to information dissemination.

The ethical obligations of ghostwriters:
Ethics are essential to ghostwriting since the
The nature of the profession necessitates a certain amount of secrecy and anonymity.

To keep the respect and confidence of their customers and readers, ghostwriters must abide by a set of moral standards:

1. Integrity and Openness: Ghostwriters should be transparent about their participation in and role in the writing process. They should not misrepresent themselves or their contribution to the customer or readers even when they stay anonymous.

2. Accuracy and authenticity: It's crucial for ghostwriters to faithfully convey the ideas, tone, and personality of their clients. Any factual material must be properly investigated and validated, and the content must be true to the client's views and experiences.

3. Respect for Confidentiality: In ghostwriting, confidentiality is crucial. Ghostwriters must maintain the strictest secrecy in all contacts, talks, and documents supplied by clients and must never share any sensitive information without express permission.

4. Avoiding Conflicts of Interest: Ghostwriters should use caution when taking on assignments that might lead to conflicts of interest, such as creating material that is at odds with their ideals or views.

5. Protecting Intellectual Property: Ghostwriters need to be aware of copyright regulations and show respect for the client's and any other sources' intellectual property rights.

6. Client Collaboration and Approval: The client's vision and ultimate approval should always come first, even while the ghostwriter makes original contributions. Throughout the whole process, the customer continues to be the major decision-maker.

7. Disclosure and Attribution: Ghostwriters should abide by the client's desires and properly acknowledge their contribution to the writing process in situations where disclosure is required or agreed upon, such as in academic or legal settings.

By keeping these moral obligations, ghostwriters may make sure that they conduct their business with honesty, competence, and respect for the confidence that their customers have put in them. Fostering fruitful and long-lasting ghostwriter relationships requires open communication, set expectations, and a dedication to moral behavior.

Confidentiality is Important in the Ghostwriting Relationship:

The foundation of the ghostwriting industry is confidentiality, which is crucial for both the ghostwriter and the client. When customers engage ghostwriters, they often divulge sensitive material that they want to publish under their name, including personal experiences, private ideas, and secret information. As a result, keeping customer information private is not only morally required but also legally and professionally.

Emphasizing the need for secrecy helps ghostwriters appreciate the seriousness of the confidence their customers have in them. Breach of secrecy may have serious repercussions, including harm to the client's reputation, legal troubles, a breakdown in trust, and detrimental effects on the ghostwriter's status in the industry. Ghostwriters must be aware that any violation of confidentiality may have long-lasting consequences for both the present project and their reputation as reliable authors overall.

Confidentiality and Trust Agreements:

The ghostwriter must make specific and unambiguous confidentiality agreements with their client before commencing any ghostwriting activity. The extent of secrecy, the categories of information to be safeguarded, the time frame for confidentiality, and the precautions taken to secure the client's information should all be included in these agreements.

These confidentiality agreements provide the groundwork for mutual respect and trust between the client and the ghostwriter. They reassure the customer that their private information will be treated with the highest care and confidentiality. The contracts also shield the ghostwriter from any misunderstandings or disagreements about the scope of secrecy during or after the job.

Protecting customer information

Best practices must be followed by ghostwriters to protect client information and avoid unintentional exposure. Several crucial tactics include:

1. Secure File Storage: Encrypted disks or secure, password-protected digital formats should be used to store all project-related documents and data to prevent unwanted access.

2. Limited Access: Ensuring that team members or collaborators are aware of the confidentiality standards and restricting access to the client's information to those who are directly engaged in the project.

3. After the project is finished and handed to the customer, all physical or digital records associated with it should be securely deleted or disposed of.

4. Secure Communication Channels: Refraining from utilizing insecure email or messaging services when communicating with the client and instead using platforms and solutions that provide encryption.

5. Anonymity in study: Assuring that any sources or contacts used in the study stay anonymous and that their identities are preserved if research is necessary for the project.

6. Non-Disclosure Agreements (NDAs): Some customers may require NDAs in addition to confidentiality agreements for further security. When necessary, ghostwriters should be ready to talk about and sign such agreements.

By carefully adhering to these best practices, ghostwriters may provide a secure and dependable atmosphere for their customers, enabling them to feel confident to share their thoughts and tales without worrying that their anonymity would be jeopardized.

In addition to being required by ethics, maintaining client anonymity is essential to the ghostwriting industry. Ghostwriters may develop solid trusting connections with their customers and ensure the success of the project while maintaining their professional reputation by stressing the value of secrecy, making explicit agreements, and putting best practices into effect.

Understanding intellectual property rights and copyrights:

A copyright is a legal privilege that gives the author of an original work the exclusive authority to control how it is used and distributed. It pertains to a variety of artistic mediums, such as writing, visual arts, music, and more. Copyright law is essential in defining ownership and use rights in the context of ghostwriting.

As the person who produced the piece, the ghostwriter usually retains the copyright rights when they produce material for a client. To ensure that the customer is the legitimate owner of the work, ghostwriters often transfer the copyright to the client via a written contract. It's possible that this arrangement may be spelled out in the ghostwriting contract or will be covered by a different document.

To prevent future disagreements, ghostwriters must make copyright ownership and transfer plain in their contracts. These rights must be expressly stated to guarantee that the client is free to use, publish, and distribute the work as they see appropriate and that the ghostwriter has no further claim to the material after delivery and payment.

Avoiding Plagiarism

Presenting someone else's thoughts, words, or work as your own without giving them full credit is plagiarism, a severe ethical and legal crime. The following measures must be taken by ghostwriters to prevent plagiarism in their work:

- Thorough Research: It is crucial to utilize reliable sources and to properly cite any facts or quotes while doing research to back up the client's work.

- Paraphrasing and Summarizing: When paraphrasing or summarizing material, care must be taken to preserve the original meaning and provide due credit to the source.

- Originality Verification: By using plagiarism-checking software, ghostwriters may make sure that the material they create is 100% unique and does not resemble any previously published work that is protected by copyright.

- Client Verification: Ghostwriters should request proof that any information or ideas provided by the client are either original or correctly cited in the final product.

- Citing Client Contributions: When a client offers particular ideas or information, the client should be acknowledged as the source.

The integrity of the work, the client's reputation, and the writing industry's moral standards may all be maintained by ghostwriters who adhere to these procedures.

Legal Considerations of Ghostwriting Agreements:

The rights and obligations of both the ghostwriter and the customer are outlined in detail in ghostwriting contracts. Important legal issues to take into account in ghostwriting agreements include:

➢ The kind and amount of the writing services to be delivered, the dates, and any deliverables must all be clearly defined in the project's scope.

➢ Copyright Transfer: Dealing with copyright ownership and making sure that the customer has the proper rights to the work when it is finished and paid for.

➢ Confidentiality and Non-Disclosure: Containing clauses that safeguard the privacy of the client's data and forbid the ghostwriter from revealing any secret or proprietary information.

➢ Payment Terms: Defining the structure of payment, including the total cost, the due date, and any extra costs or royalties, if any.

➢ Indemnification and Liability: Outlining each party's obligations in the event of a lawsuit or allegation of copyright infringement or defamation.

➢ Establishing processes for project termination, revisions, and the management of subpar work are all part of the termination and revisions category.

➤ Dispute Resolution: Including a procedure for addressing conflicts that might develop during the project.

Before signing, it is critical for all parties to carefully analyze the contract and, if required, obtain legal counsel. A well-written contract lays the groundwork for a fruitful and expert working relationship by guaranteeing that both the ghostwriter and the customer are safeguarded.

The ethics code for ghostwriters

The professional behavior of ghostwriters is governed by a set of guiding principles known as the "Ghostwriter's Code of Ethics." It defines the moral principles they promise to observe while dealing with customers and writing content. When considering a ghostwriter's code of ethics, there are two key factors to take into account: already-existing standards from professional bodies and organizations, and the creation of a personal code of ethics.

Existing Codes of Ethics: There may be established codes of ethics that members are urged or expected to abide by in professional groups and organizations relating to writing, publishing, and ghostwriting. These codes are often created to provide a structure for moral conduct, encouraging responsibility and trust within the sector. They could talk about things like conflicts of interest, plagiarism, attribution, and secrecy when it comes to ghostwriting.

For ghostwriters looking to better grasp the ethics and standards of the field, investigating current codes of ethics may be an invaluable exercise. Ghostwriters may show their dedication to professionalism and link themselves with the larger community of writing professionals by upholding these recognized norms.

Personal Code of Ethics: Ghostwriters must create their code of ethics in addition to abiding by external regulations. This unique collection of rules is a reflection of the person's moral principles, values, and worldview. When confronted with moral conundrums peculiar to their particular projects and clientele, it may serve as a moral compass, directing decision-making.

Ghostwriters can match their work with their own moral principles and professional objectives by encouraging them to create a personal code of ethics. Their code should be built on values like honesty, decency, confidentiality of clients, and commitment to creating high-quality work.

Integrating Personal and Existing Ethics:

The Ghostwriter's Code of Ethics should be consistent with both current industry standards and the ghostwriter's moral principles. A personal code allows for unique reflection and modification to particular client demands and projects, whereas professional codes provide a conventional baseline. For instance, a ghostwriter's code can include providing credit to all contributors to the project if a professional organization promotes correct attribution and prevents plagiarism. This can be given due recognition to co-authors, researchers, or subject-matter experts who contributed their knowledge to the work.

Additionally, a ghostwriter's code may include provisions for openness and communication, ensuring that customers are completely informed of the ghostwriting procedure and any possible restrictions or difficulties that may emerge during the project.

In the end, a thorough Ghostwriter's Code of Ethics equips professionals to do excellent work while maintaining a strong sense of duty and integrity. It emphasizes the significance of moral behavior throughout the ghostwriting process, establishing client trust, and protecting the standing of the ghostwriting industry as a whole. Ghostwriters may increase their reputation, create enduring connections with customers, and positively impact the writing and publishing industries by following these guidelines.

Ghostwriting and Ethics in Different Industries:

➤ Literary ghostwriting: Writing novels, memoirs, or other literary works on behalf of famous people, public personalities, or other people who do not have the time, writing talent, or knowledge to do so themselves is known as literary ghostwriting. Transparency, authenticity, and the delicate balancing act between the ghostwriter's creative contribution and the subject's voice are the key ethical issues in this field.

➤ Transparency and authenticity: Upholding readers' trust is one of the fundamental ethical issues in literary ghostwriting. Readers sometimes think that the author of a book who publishes it under the name of a famous person or public figure created it themselves. Although ghostwriting is a regular activity, it calls into doubt the authorship's veracity. A degree of transparency that honors readers' expectations while preserving the subject's privacy must be decided upon between the ghostwriter and the subject.

➤ Maintaining the Subject's Voice: A talented literary ghostwriter must establish a balance between their literary prowess and the subject's distinctive voice and personality. The objective is to authentically convey the subject's tone, ideas, and experiences while making sure the writing is strong and engaging. Maintaining the subject's voice is crucial for establishing confidence between the subject and the readers as well as from an ethical standpoint.

➤ Ethical Limits: When the subject wishes to incorporate sensitive or contentious material, literary ghostwriters may run into ethical problems. It takes careful study and discussion between the ghostwriter and the client to strike a balance between the subject's desire for candor and any possible legal or reputational repercussions.

College ghostwriting

➤ Writing academic papers, essays, theses, or dissertations for students or academics is known as academic ghostwriting. As it violates the values of academic honesty and integrity, this practice raises serious ethical questions in the academic world.

➢ **Academic Integrity:** Honesty, creativity, and appropriate idea credit are the cornerstones of academia. By passing off someone else's work as the student's own, academic ghostwriting compromises these values and results in academic dishonesty.

➢ **Unfair edge:** Using ghostwritten academic material gives users an unfair edge. Bypassing the educational process denies children the chance to study and develop their critical thinking, research, and knowledge abilities.

➢ **Education-Related Consequences**: The ubiquity of academic ghostwriting may diminish the value of education and academic credentials.

If institutions are linked to academic dishonesty, their reputation may suffer and the worth of their degrees may decline.

Corporate ghostwriting:

➢ Writing content for firms or executives, such as speeches, articles, blog posts, marketing materials, or internal communications, is known as business ghostwriting. Authenticity, truthfulness, and correctly portraying the company's principles and ethics are all ethical issues in this field.

➢ Representing Company Values: Honest business ghostwriters need to make sure that the material they produce complies with the organization's ethics, purpose, and core values. They should avoid producing false or misleading information that might damage the reputation of the business or mislead consumers.

➢ Accurate material: Before using any material in any article, business ghostwriters should meticulously fact-check and validate it. Building audience trust and preserving the company's reputation depends on the presentation of correct facts and information.

➢ Creating convincing writing that promotes a company's goods or services while being honest with the audience is a delicate balance that ethical business ghostwriters must strike. For ethical business ghostwriting, avoiding fraudulent advertising or misleading claims is essential.

In ghostwriting for many sectors, ethics are essential. Ghostwriters must traverse difficult ethical issues while producing everything from literary masterpieces to academic papers and business material to guarantee openness, authenticity, and integrity. For ethical issues to be resolved and material to be produced that upholds the values and expectations of all parties involved, communication and cooperation between ghostwriters and clients are essential.

How to Respond to Unethical Requests:

Making Ethical Decisions:

When customers seek acts or material that clash with their principles, professional standards, or legal requirements, ghostwriters often find themselves in difficult ethical situations. To retain one's integrity and respect the ethical standards of one's trade, the ghostwriter must make ethical decisions in such circumstances. The following outline will help ghostwriters as they assess and react to unethical requests:

Define the Ethical Issue: To start, decide what the current ethical issue is. Find out whatever particular component of the request creates ethical concerns and why it is an issue.

Understand Relevant Guidelines: Become familiar with the professional standards, legal regulations, and industry ethics that are relevant to your job as a ghostwriter. You can contextualize the circumstance and find probable infractions with the aid of this step.

Consider Consequences: Consider the possible repercussions of granting the unethical request. Aside from the immediate effects on your customer connection, think about the bigger picture effects on your reputation, career, and the industry as a whole.

Consult with Coworkers or Mentors: Ask coworkers, mentors, or organizations for professional advice and direction. Participating in conversations with others may provide insightful and insightful viewpoints that may help you make a better-educated choice.

Consider your own beliefs and ethical standards when you assess your values. Think about whether your choice is consistent with your integrity and whether you would be at ease with the results of accepting or declining the request.

Communicate Clearly: If you are unsure if a request is morally acceptable, instantly talk to your customer. Be open to examining other options and clearly state your objections and justifications for refusing the request.

Managing Complex Ethical Conundrums:

➢ Examples of difficult ethical decisions made in the real world might provide helpful advice on how ghostwriters can handle tricky circumstances while upholding their ethical standards. Here are some examples of circumstances and possible strategies:

> Ghostwriting Controversial or False Information: A customer requests you to create material that disseminates false information or advances opinions that you find objectionable. You may politely refuse the assignment in this case by stating that it conflicts with your moral principles and dedication to truth.

> Request for Plagiarism or Unauthorized Use of Material: A customer requests that you omit the required credit when using information from copyrighted sources. Inform the customer about the value of copyright and intellectual property rights in this situation, and provide other methods for producing unique material.

> A customer asks you to ghostwrite a book without mentioning that you did so, giving

readers the impression that the author did all the writing on their own. Here, you may promote openness by arguing that sincerity and authenticity are essential for winning readers' confidence.

➤ Writing Academic Papers for Students: When a student asks you to write their academic paper for them, academic integrity concerns are raised. Refuse the request politely and recommend that they look for help from genuine academic resources like tutoring or writing centers.

➤ Balancing customer's Desires with Ethical Concerns: A customer asks for a narrative that unfairly favors them, yet doing so can distort the truth or jeopardize the credibility of the tale. In this situation, express the value of being loyal to the narrative's core while taking the client's wish for a favorable representation into account.

Ghostwriters have an inherent obstacle when dealing with immoral demands, but by developing a strong foundation for ethical judgment and learning from actual cases, they may handle these circumstances with professionalism and honesty. Ghostwriters may retain their reputation, develop lasting client relationships, and positively impact the writing and publishing industries by adhering to ethical norms.

CHAPTER 5

FINDING OPPORTUNITIES AS A GHOSTWRITER

Best locations to look for ghostwriting work;
Find profitable and desirable assignments while looking for ghostwriting chances. Concentrate on marketing your services in person, online, or by looking for possibilities on reputable ghostwriter platforms. The following are some of the top locations to look for ghostwriting jobs:

Upwork
Online freelancing marketplace Upwork has a ton of options for ghostwriting. Regardless of your level of experience, you're likely to discover a project that works for you. Invitations from customers continue to be free even if Upwork costs you to submit a proposal for a job posting.

Fiverr

You may sell your services on Fiverr's site. In essence, you have the freedom to establish your fees for your ghostwriter services and construct gig packages with several levels. Since the customers come directly to you on this site, it is very helpful for ghostwriters who don't want to spend time placing bids on new jobs.

FlexJobs

FlexJobs is a website for remote employment that provides several options for ghostwriting. Its objective is to provide top-notch remote employment that is flexible, which is ideal for ghostwriters. You may access free educational tools like webinars and skills tests on the website as well.

HireWriters

Consider utilizing HireWriters if you want to locate ghostwriting gigs rapidly. On HireWriters, which is geared at independent writers, you may choose your rates. You may not initially locate high-paying employment on HireWriters, but with time, you can come across worthwhile tasks there.

Verblio

Verblio offers authors the chance to work for money. There is a network of authors searching for employment on the internet. The ideal writer is then matched with a company wishing to employ someone who can write for their specialty via Verblio. Bloggers and website owners both post job openings on their sites. New job openings are updated frequently on the website itself.

Here are some effective strategies for breaking into the field of ghostwriting and finding those well-paying assignments:

➢ Establish relationships: The majority of customers who are willing to spend a considerable amount of money to hire a ghostwriter for a book will want a reference or referral from a reliable source. It is crucial to start networking and publicizing your ghostwriter services because of this. Attend networking events, become more involved in your community (locally and online!), build relationships with other authors and editors, and widen your circle of influence to discover high-paying ghostwriting gigs.

➢ Use your knowledge to dominate a market niche: Utilize your present knowledge and expertise. If you work as a career coach, you are in a good position to write for a client who wants to publish a book about their career. You would be a fantastic ghostwriter for a sports personality if you have experience writing sports pieces. The same is true whether you have any commercial, legal, or medical expertise. Discover customers in such areas by using your knowledge. Many businessmen, attorneys, and professionals would want to write a book but lack the time. You fill that role, of course!

➤ Use your present clients, editors, and recommendations. If you're a freelance writer, you probably already have relationships in the publishing industry. Utilize your present "clients" to get recommendations for prospective ghostwriter customers and business prospects. Getting recommendations is a crucial part of finding prospective "authors."

➤ Utilize Internet marketing: There are several free and inexpensive methods to sell and advertise your ghostwriting services online. Go to writing-related websites like WritersDigest.com, WritersMarket.com, or Mediabistro.com. These and other websites provide tools, lessons, connections, and information to help you write more quickly. Launch your website or blog to promote your services as well.

Follow the ghost trail: Leads and recommendations may also be found by talking to other authors and ghostwriters. Partner up with other writers and offer to take on their "extra" clients as ghostwriters often only have time to work with one or two clients at once. You may even pay the writer your "sub-contract" with a finder's fee.

You'll be successful as a ghostwriter if you follow these tips!

Getting Started as a Ghostwriter

Being a competent writer and listener are prerequisites for working as a ghostwriter. A talented ghostwriter may record their client's voice so that the words on the page "sound" like them while they are speaking.

If you think you'd be a good match for this line of employment, think about doing these actions:

Select the Proper Location

The majority of American publishers, including those that need ghostwriting services, have their headquarters in New York City. But living in New York specifically isn't the secret to a successful ghostwriting business. It involves having access to the kind of persons that need book ghostwriting.

Create a Network

So how can you get these prospective customers' attention? There is no doubting the potential benefits of human connections. If you network with the right people, word of mouth may get out to prospective clients who are seeking for ghostwriting services.

Request recommendations

It's also crucial to let folks know that you're looking for ghostwriting work right now. Word-of-mouth has a strong track record of changing people's behaviors, but this only works if your social networks are aware of what you intend to accomplish. Make your goals known to those who have links to the publishing sector in particular. If you know a freelance editor or an accomplished author, they could recommend you. Publishing firms often suggest ghostwriters to renowned people whose memoir rights they have just acquired.

Improve Your Craft

Hard effort may also go you far if you lack social ties. Getting writing examples out there is the most crucial thing you can do. One option to achieve this is to self-publish your books. You may start a blog or create a podcast series of your own. Whatever the format, keep in mind that writing assignments under your name may help you get those under someone else's name.

Improve Your Interviewing Techniques

The customary when beginning a ghostwriting assignment is for the writer and their clients to have lengthy interviews.

 In certain instances, the credited author and the ghostwriter lay out the main points of each chapter as they go through the whole intended book. Some subjects may even go farther since they are aware that their name is on the byline; as a consequence, they may have specific drafting and editing suggestions.

Create Your Style

One assignment may rapidly lead to more recommendations, so if you can establish your brand with a certain publishing house or within a network of people (such as actors or sportsmen), you can earn an entire career out of ghostwriting books If you can, continue allocating up time for projects that you write in your manner. You can balance both a personal writing style and a ghostwriting approach while continuing to enjoy the financial and creative benefits of doing so.

CHAPTER 6

WRITING ACROSS GENRES

Understanding the differences between genres

Defining genres and their distinctive features

According to their substance, style, and topics, comparable works are grouped under certain categories or classifications called genres. Every genre has certain characteristics that set it different from others. For instance, whereas science fiction digs into speculative technology and future locations, romance books often concentrate on love and relationships. To successfully negotiate the complexities of each genre, a ghostwriter must have a solid understanding of these distinguishing traits.

Analyzing the target market for each genre reveals that different genres appeal to distinct markets with unique tastes and demands. It is crucial to identify the key reader demographic for each genre to adjust the material. Young adult literature, for instance, focuses on adolescent readers coping with coming-of-age themes, while self-help books are written with readers wanting personal growth and development in mind. To produce interesting and accessible material, ghostwriters must take the target audience's hobbies, age range, and cultural background into account.

Different genres' tones, styles, and customs should be recognized:

The reader's experience is shaped by the particular tone and style of each genre. For instance, the tone in a thriller may be strong and suspenseful, yet in a comedy, it might be lighthearted and amusing. In addition, readers anticipate certain genre-specific tropes. For instance, although fantasy stories often have magical aspects and heroic journeys, mystery novels generally feature a crime, a detective, and a conclusion. To maintain authenticity and live up to readers' expectations, ghostwriters need to be knowledgeable about certain genre-specific components.

A ghostwriter must be knowledgeable about the variations between genres to specialize in one genre or move fluidly between others. Ghostwriters may produce engrossing and genuine works that engage with readers and satisfy the needs of the publishing business by defining genres, examining target demographics, and establishing tone, style, and conventions. A talented ghostwriter modifies their writing abilities to meet the distinctive qualities of each genre, whether they are writing romance, mystery, fantasy, or any other, delivering a captivating and enjoyable reading experience for the audience.

For ghostwriters, the ability to adapt effortlessly between several genres while keeping a high standard of quality in their work is an essential talent. An in-depth examination of this subtopic is provided below:

Writing Style Modification for Different Genres:

Each genre has certain demands and traits of its own. For instance, the writing style of a mystery or fantasy book will be quite different from that of a romance novel. The intricacies of each genre must be understood by ghostwriters to successfully modify their writing style.

It's crucial to comprehend the pace, tone, and narrative structure common to many genres. For instance, literary fiction could place more of an emphasis on introspection and character development than a thriller, which calls for a quick-paced, exciting writing style.

Ghostwriters may write more convincingly by immersing themselves in the language and culture of the chosen genre via intensive research and reading.

Keeping the Authorial Voice While Adhering to the requirements of the Genre:

The ghostwriter must keep the author's distinctive voice even while writing in a new genre since every author has one. Readers should not get the impression that they are reading anything altogether new when they do this.

Finding a good balance between the author's voice and the requirements of the genre is difficult. Finding a balance between the author's natural style and the genre's stylistic standards is something that ghostwriters may do. Maintaining consistency and authenticity may be made easier by working closely with the author, grasping their vision, and asking for input as you go.

"Depending on the genre, knowing whether to be more formal or informal".

Different genres need different degrees of formality in writing. For example, academic or historical genres could call for a more formal tone, but contemporary literature often favors a more casual, conversational style. The importance of dialogue in determining formality or informality cannot be overstated. Ghostwriters may create genuine and acceptable speech by taking into account the characters' origins, social position, and personality.

To make reading enjoyable for the audience and increase their connection with the tale, the degree of formality should be balanced properly.

Ghostwriters need to constantly practice, read extensively, and be open to criticism if they want to perfect the skill of changing their writing style to fit different genres. Writing requires flexibility and variety to bring out the best in each project and meet the unique demands of both writers and readers. Ghostwriters may greatly contribute to the success of many genres and increase their career chances in the publishing industry by expertly modifying their writing style.

The Dos and Don'ts of Genre Combination

Recognize Why Genre Matters: Blended-genre novels are a popular trend right now, but to pull one off well, you must first comprehend the fundamental characteristics of genre fiction. The Oxford English Dictionary claims that the word genre, which in French means "a kind," was borrowed from the Latin word genera, which in scientific parlance is a category that shares a set of related characteristics. Just as scientists want to know if they are dealing with an animal, vegetable, or mineral, we label novels as mystery, romance, fantasy, and other similar categories in publishing.

Genre is mostly a marketing strategy; "It's a category marker that tells us in which section of the bookstore your book will be sold."
You must be conscious of your audience while writing as a result. Where would your target reader look at the bookshop to find books similar to yours? You may not be able to answer the first questions while you write, such as the specific subgenre your novel belongs to (more on that in a moment). By doing this, you'll get a step closer to determining where your book fits in and a step closer to getting it there.

Genre is all about what the viewer expects to see. By definition, genres adhere to a formula, and readers often confess that knowing what that formula is gives them comfort. For a certain form of escape, whether it's solving a mystery, becoming lost in a new universe, or being sucked into a romance, genre readers turn to their books. Knowing the guidelines is crucial if you want to write genre fiction that appeals to these people. And being one of those readers is the greatest way to do it. Reading similar novels can offer you a better understanding of the genre's norms, help you determine where your narrative fits in, and provide you with a library of comparative books to use in your inquiry when the time comes.

The Base Genre Is Identity

Let's use the recipe comparison from the opening question of this post as our starting point (this is a pretty popular strategy, and I will confess that I do not enjoy it). When making soup, several different components are included. The soup itself, however, doesn't taste exactly like everything. With soup, there is a foundation taste that the additional components serve to accentuate. And that's how you go about fusing genres: There has to be a basis, first and foremost. Mystery, romance, fantasy, science fiction, literature, horror, historical fiction, thriller, comedy, and drama are the most widely read genres. Choosing the ideal place for your narrative to fit should be your first step.

Start by asking yourself this important question: What is the storyline of your narrative based on? This will help you choose your base—your emphasis. Is it centered on two characters developing a love relationship? Is the main focus on catching the murderer? Is it centered on a conflict between two mythical creatures?

Add an equal amount of each genre.

Any items you add should enhance, not dominate, your foundation. Remember that even while your narrative could include aspects of a romance, a murder mystery, and a new fantasy world, it doesn't always imply it fits into all three genres. A competent chef understands that not everything tastes well together. Which one should be the attention, you have to decide? Where in the bookshop are books like yours stocked?

Your book can't be in two places at once, and knowing where it will probably end up might help you better understand your target audience.

Subgenres may be defined by secondary elements.

Of course, not all tales can be neatly classified into the main genres, which is why there are subgenres.

While certain subgenres, such as the division of humor into satire or parody, often develop into their distinct genres, for the sake of this article, we'll concentrate on those that are created through blending several genres. Popular genres include literary horror, dark drama, magical realism, chick-lit, romantic suspense, supernatural thriller, historical romance, and paranormal mystery. In these subgenres, the first word is a descriptive term describing the book within that larger category, while the second word represents the base genre.

For instance, if the central conflict of your story is the question of "will they or won't they?"that, like J.R. " that keeps romance fans on the edge of their seats. The genre is mostly romance, as shown in books like Ward's Black Dagger Brotherhood or Gena Showalter's Lords of the Underworld trilogy. The other components are what distinguish these novels as paranormal romances, one of the most popular subgenres right now. The novel on your computer is a romance even if the werewolf pack's escape is crucial to your hero and heroine ultimately getting together. If the plot can't be regarded as complete without the couple getting together. The supernatural components improve your basic materials.

Let's examine an additional, gaining in popularity subgenre, urban fantasy. The world-building and the conflict that take place in that imagined world take center stage in Jim Butcher's The Dresden Files, Kim Harrison's The Hollows books, and other works in this category. The setting, which may have a huge impact on your characters and plot, is secondary. The same goes for every relationship, even if it's a crucial one.

Impose a genre

Despite all of this, there may still be a lot of gray areas when it comes to mixing genres (and here is the point when you detest the publishing business and its fussy ways!). Take the popular book Bitten by Kelley Armstrong as an example. The relationship, which starts as a side storyline, ends up being one of the most important aspects of how the tale is resolved. As a result of the detailed world-building, Bitten sometimes reads more like a paranormal coming-of-age novel than a standard paranormal romance. There are exceptions to every norm in publishing, as there always are.

However, in general, publications with clearly defined categories are simpler to sell since publishers are better equipped to assess and serve the market for such works. However, don't give up if you honestly don't know how your book fits in. Just put pen to paper and create the greatest possible narrative you can. If you're hesitant or confused when it comes to pitching editors and agents, like my mother always said, "When in doubt, leave it out."

Patrick Lee, the bestselling author of the supernatural thriller The Breach and a rookie author, didn't assign a genre to his book when he sent a query to Janet Reid of FinePrint Literary Management. "He didn't talk to me about genre," claims Reid. The genre component came later, and that's OK, "He talked to me about an engaging story." Instead of pitching a book that an author has attempted to pass off as something it is not, agents would like to learn about a wonderful tale. They'll assist in deciding where your book belongs when the time comes if they have strong feelings about it.

Leave the Final Decision to the Experts

Let's assume that you've done your research and identified your base genre and subcategory. You may be surprised to learn that, after you've polished the tale, signed with an agent, and sold it to a publisher, the sales and marketing divisions of the latter are ultimately responsible for formally categorizing your book. (This is the other point when you detest publishing and all its demands!) So why categorize it in the first place if someone may modify it later? Again, the simpler something is to understand, the more likely it is to sell—and that begins with you.

The publicists and booksellers are assisting you in reaching your audience once your book has been categorized, released, and stocked. And booksellers are the best people to ask about audience expectations.

There are equally strong arguments for shelving Charlaine Harris' Sookie Stackhouse books in speculative fiction, paranormal, or even urban fantasy, but we still do so, says Maryelizabeth Hart, co-owner and publicity manager for San Diego's Mysterious Galaxy Books.

Hart observes how her clients browse for books and adjust the shelf as necessary. The mystery reader base has responded well to a lot of our paranormal publications, she continues. The book's framework is solidly rooted in the mystery genre, but it has recently been enhanced by the [paranormal] aspect, written by writers Victoria Laurie and Juliet Blackwell.

This supports the notion that deciding on a basic flavor, or emphasis, is essential for connecting with your target audience.

Prioritize the story

Although blending genres is popular right now, the idea is not new. Additionally, a book may still find a publisher even if it doesn't cleanly fall into a certain category. In actuality, new subgenres continue to emerge. I'm fortunate enough to work with Nancy

Coffey, who, as an editor at Avon in the 1970s, effectively contributed to the creation of the historical romance genre. The number of historical novels with female protagonists was lower back then than it is today, and with a few notable exceptions, the great majority of these works were gothic romances. by Kathleen E. "The Flame and the Flower" Woodiwiss then appeared. It was simpler to convince the sales staff that this was something fresh and had never been attempted back then, according to Coffey.

Still, it's a possibility. It may be harder than ever to figure out where you belong now since there are so many subgenres and creative combinations that use anything from visual elements, as in Jeff Kinney's Diary of a Wimpy Kid, to poetry, as in Ellen Hopkins' Crank.

How can you know when you've effectively merged genres when you have all of this to consider?

I've worked with clients who weren't sure how their work would fit in the market, but I still signed them because of how effectively they presented their tales. Because, as I previously said, a strong tale is ultimately what counts the most. Without it, your book won't sell, regardless of its category or subgenre.

Try not to shoehorn your work into a certain genre or subgenre just because it's the hottest thing right now. The newly incorporated components must contribute to the plot for it to be enhanced. Readers want their cross-genre elements to have a purpose, according to Hart.

Be conscious of audience expectations, but not to the point that they override the need to tell the tale. Even if we editors and agents appreciate your market and audience understanding, as the writer, it isn't your main concern. The tale you are dying to write should be your priority.

CHAPTER 7

THE NEED FOR RESEARCH AND FACT CHECKING

It's essential to develop your research and fact-checking abilities for all writing and academic endeavors, not just ghostwriting. The following advice can help you improve your skills in these areas:

➤ Realize its significance: Understand the importance of research and fact-checking in creating dependable and accurate material. Internalize the duty you have as a writer to provide your audience with accurate and reliable information.

➤ Use reliable sources: Only depend on reliable, knowledgeable sources while doing your study. In general, academic journals, official reports, peer-reviewed papers, and reputable media sources are more trustworthy than personal blogs or unreliable websites.

➤ Cross-reference data: When doing research, confirm the data from several sources. Comparing data from several reliable sources will help you see any possible biases or mistakes and improve the trustworthiness of your work.

➤ Develop your capacity to critically evaluate information by honing your critical thinking abilities. Analyze the evidence provided in the sources you come across, challenge the veracity of assertions, and look out for logical fallacies.

➤ Stay current: Information changes quickly, particularly in certain industries. Keep up with the most recent alterations, discoveries, and advancements in the fields you write about.

➢ Check your facts carefully: No matter how reliable the material in your article may appear, you should always double-check it. Pay close attention to the little details and make sure that every assertion is supported by reliable data.

➢ Use the information and tools for fact-checking that are accessible online. FactCheck.org, Snopes, and Politifact are a few websites that may assist you in checking the veracity of assertions and dispelling widespread fallacies.

➢ Learn from criticism: If you get comments or corrections on your work, use the chance to grow. Make a mental note of the mistakes committed and strive to avoid making the same ones in the future.

➢ Develop effective research techniques: Improve your research techniques by understanding how to utilize sophisticated search operators, efficiently traverse databases, and navigate libraries.

➢ Maintain a record of your sources and arrange your research notes carefully. This helps you keep a clear perspective of your study and makes it simpler to go back to the data when necessary.

➢ Seek mentoring and advice from seasoned writers, researchers, or subject matter experts who can provide insightful criticism and assist you in honing your research and fact-checking methods.

➢ Practice frequently: Consistent practice is crucial for learning any skill. Set goals for yourself to write on a variety of subjects, do extensive research and carefully verify your sources.

You'll not only become a more trustworthy and credible writer by using these tactics and making a commitment to developing your research and fact-checking abilities, but you'll also support the spread of correct information at a time when dependable content is highly prized.

While there are valid uses for ghostwriting, such as assisting busy or inexperienced people to express their thoughts clearly, it also raises serious questions about the need for research and fact-checking.

➢ Credibility: Ensuring the end product's credibility is one of the main issues with ghostwriting. Whether it's a book or a public speech, when someone signs their name to it, they are effectively confirming its veracity and authenticity. If the text includes errors, exaggerations, or sloppy research, it not only harms the author's reputation but also erodes the confidence of the audience or readers.

➤ Readers and content consumers look for accuracy and authenticity in their material. They depend on the material to be trustworthy and factually accurate whether it is in a non-fiction book, a research paper, or a blog post. Therefore, to guarantee that the material they produce satisfies these standards, ghostwriters must do extensive research and fact-checking.

➤ Ethics: Ghostwriting may muddy the boundaries between authorship and present moral dilemmas. It is often believed that when someone is listed as the author, they actively contribute to the writing. Although the contribution of the ghostwriter is often recognized, this is not always the case. To authentically convey the author's thoughts and maintain ethical openness in such circumstances, the ghostwriter must do thorough research.

➢ Legal repercussions: In certain instances, unreliable or copied material in a ghostwritten work may give rise to legal challenges. The repercussions might be severe if the credited author is accused of plagiarizing or spreading misleading material. Correct fact-checking and research may reduce these dangers and protect both the author and the ghostwriter.

➢ Impact on readers and society: Whether deliberate or accidental, misinformation may harm both readers and society at large. Unchecked facts may lead to the propagation of misconceptions, misunderstandings, and even public damage in the information era, as content travels quickly. This duty falls on the shoulders of the ghostwriters, who must carefully research the data they use in their writing.

➢ Building experience and knowledge: Ghostwriting gives authors the chance to dig into a variety of themes and topics. Proper research and fact-checking not only guarantee the content's correctness but also provide the ghostwriter the chance to expand their knowledge and experience across a range of subjects, strengthening their writing skills.

In ghostwriting, thorough investigation and fact-checking are essential. It preserves the end product's integrity, authenticity, and ethics; it shields the author and the ghostwriter from legal repercussions; and, most significantly, it makes sure that readers get accurate and truthful information. Ghostwriters may help the spread of reliable and worthwhile work in the literary community and beyond by adopting a strict approach to research and fact-checking.

CHAPTER 8

MANAGING GHOSTWRITING AGREEMENT

To guarantee a smooth and fruitful cooperation between the author (the person who hires the ghostwriter) and the ghostwriter, managing a ghostwriting agreement is crucial. A well-structured agreement safeguards the interests of both parties, establishes obligations, and puts forward clear expectations. Here is a thorough guide on handling a ghostwriting contract:

✓ Clear Communication: The cornerstone of every successful ghostwriting endeavor is honest and open communication. Discuss the project's objectives, timetable, and any unique needs or preferences, as well as its scope. Before moving forward, make sure that everyone is aware of one another's expectations and agrees.

✓ Describe Project Scope: The agreement should expressly describe the project's scope. Give a brief description of the sort of material that will be created (such as a book, article, or speech), its planned length, and any extra services like research, editing, or revisions.

✓ Confidentiality and non-disclosure: When ghostwriting, sensitive or private information is often involved. Incorporate a secrecy provision into the contract to safeguard the author's thoughts, private information, and any unpublished works.

✓ Copyright and Ownership: Specify who owns the rights to the work in the agreement. The acknowledged author often keeps the copyright, while the ghostwriter is compensated for their efforts. Determine if the ghostwriter will be given any credit or acknowledgment for their work.

✓ Describe the payment arrangements, including the overall remuneration, the timing of payments, and any upfront costs or milestones. Indicate the payment method and how any extra costs will be handled.

✓ Schedule and Deadlines: Come to an understanding of a reasonable schedule for the project and establish firm deadlines for deliveries. This makes sure that everyone is informed of the anticipated advancement and finish dates.

✓ Revision and Editing Process: Specify the procedure for requesting and executing modifications, as well as the number of revisions covered under the agreement. This ensures that the final product fits the author's expectations and helps avoid misconceptions regarding the extent of modifications.

✓ Include a termination provision that specifies the circumstances under which any party may end the agreement. Deal with problems including missed deadlines, contract violations, or other unanticipated events.

✓ Legal and Jurisdiction: Indicate the laws and jurisdictions that will be used to interpret and execute the agreement. When working with customers or ghostwriters from other nations or states, this is very crucial.

✓ Communication and Availability: Specify your expectations for your level of availability and communication frequency. To keep a process efficient, decide on preferred communication routes and reaction times.

✓ Sample Work and Portfolio: The ghostwriter may, if appropriate, insert a provision enabling them to utilize the finished product as part of their portfolio or for self-promotion.

✓ Review of the Contract: Have a lawyer examine the contract to make sure it is enforceable and safeguards the interests of both parties.

✓ Signatures: To make the agreement legally enforceable, both parties must sign it when all terms have been agreed upon.

✓ Establish a clear communication procedure for managing any problems or difficulties that could come up throughout the project. The chosen means of communication, the conflict resolution procedure through escalation, and the designated point of contact for each party should all be included in this protocol.

✓ The significance of thorough research and fact-checking in the ghostwriting process should be emphasized. Clearly state that the ghostwriter will do thorough research to verify the authenticity and trustworthiness of the text.

✓ Handling Revisions: Describe the procedure for dealing with corrections and criticism. Set a deadline for when modifications should be sought and handled. To avoid too much back and forth, all sides should agree on a fair amount of modifications.

✓ Payment and Invoicing: Specify how payments are made and how often invoices are sent. Indicate the payment method, such as a bank transfer, PayPal, or another safe way. Clarify the invoice delivery information as well as the time range for payment when milestones are reached.

✓ Intellectual Property Rights: Address any such rights about the created material. The author must have the freedom to use the work in any way they see fit, and the ghostwriter must have no ownership or control over the material once the job is over.

✓ Conflicts of Interest: Resolve any possible conflicts that could develop during the project. Any connections or relationships that can skew the content's impartiality or integrity should be disclosed by both parties.

✓ Include a section that specifies the process for resolving disputes, such as mediation or arbitration, to avoid the need for legal action between the author and the ghostwriter.

✓ Indicate each party's obligations about any possible legal claims or liabilities resulting from the substance in the indemnification clause.

Both parties benefit from indemnification provisions since they shield them from any legal repercussions brought on by the other party's acts or inactions.

✓ Rights and Citations: If the project calls for the use of copyrighted materials, make sure the necessary rights are secured and the content is properly cited. In the agreement, it should be stated who is responsible for securing these authorizations and citations.

✓ Clarify if the ghostwriter must maintain the project's confidentiality even after it is finished, particularly if the author intends to publish or make the work publicly known.

✓ Include terms for contract renewal or extension, as well as any applicable revised conditions, if there is a chance that the partnership may continue beyond the original project.

✓ Post-Project Support: Describe any post-project assistance the ghostwriter could provide, such as assisting with advertising materials or responding to concerns about the content.

CHAPTER 9

CREATING YOUR GHOSTWRITING PORTFOLIO

Many freelance writers have difficulties establishing their reputations, but ghostwriters may face difficulties that are considerably more pronounced.

Fortunately, there are several legal methods to demonstrate your credentials and expertise to build a ghostwriting portfolio. In this essay, we'll look at 4 of such approaches.

How to Build a Portfolio for Ghostwriting

Testimonials Should Be Featured on Your Website

I don't know about you, but when I purchase on Amazon, even if two products have the same overall rating, I'm more inclined to choose the one with 200 favorable ratings than the one with 3.

Even if those hopeful thoughts come from strangers, there is something about seeing a flurry of them that compels me to take out my credit card. Accuse me of being gullible, but I'm not the only one. In fact, according to 50% of Americans, word-of-mouth recommendations are the sole source of advertising information they would prefer.

This is only one of several data that demonstrate the effectiveness of word-of-mouth marketing.

The phrase "social proof" was initially used to describe this phenomenon by author Robert Cialdini in his 1984 book Influence. It conveys the concept that people and organizations will adjust their actions to fit public opinion in a certain circumstance.

In light of this, ghostwriters would be wise to develop and maintain a database of customer reviews, which serve as an excellent source of social proof.

Testimonials confirm your authorship and provide potential customers confidence by proving that others have trusted you in the past and had positive results.

Even delighted customers may not be willing to provide these testimonials, so don't rely on luck to get them. Send an email to your writer's website when a job is finished requesting for a review to appear there.

Even better, you may include a (polite) language in your contracts indicating that, as long as the task is done well, a recommendation will count toward your needed payment. Although it may sound confrontational, it is a frequent tactic.

An excerpt is a brief passage of text taken from a larger body of writing.

A few small, esoteric lines from a book or scientific article you wrote for someone, for instance, may be shown in your portfolio.

There are a few significant points to remember about this.

First and foremost, it's important to conduct yourself professionally; be honest with your customers and do not act secretly.

Another area where you need to be extremely precise in your contracts is the authority to utilize extracts. Have that conversation at the absolute least, and put it in writing—even if it's just an email.

Explain what information you will utilize and how you will use it to allay any anxieties they may have.

Second, don't take more text than is necessary to show new customers what you can achieve without taking away from your present clients' revenues. Depending on the length and complexity of the final product, as well as your client's comfort level, it should be feasible to achieve this in just a few words at most.

Make Test Articles Your Models

As independent contractors, we are all familiar with the routine: often, a potential client will ask you to create a little piece gratis so they can assess your suitability to write for them.

Although this might be annoying, it seems sensible that they would want to evaluate your skills while minimizing their risk. However, you may also take advantage of this. You may gather these items to present prospective clients as long as they are just being used for testing and not, for instance, to be published on their website.

Although there shouldn't be any issues with this, you should still be honest with anybody who requests a free sample piece. Freelancing may be risky, therefore the more transparent you are about your business procedures, the less likely you are to run into problems.

A Ghostwriting Blog

Create a blog to demonstrate your skills as a ghostwriter. You may use your own experience when giving advice to others who are in a similar situation to you (while maintaining confidentiality, of course).

Here are some suggestions for blog topics to use:
- ✓ How to Set Your Rates as a Ghostwriter
- ✓ How to Legally Protect Yourself
- ✓ Why Ghostwriting Is a Great Career

- ✓ How to Change Your Writing Voice to Suit Your Client
- ✓ 8 Things to Do in Your First Month as a Ghostwriter.
- ✓ The Following 5 Books Will Improve Your Ghostwriting Skills

Recall how we discussed social proof.

Additionally, fostering constructive debates in the comments area is a terrific approach to increase trust. Responding to inquiries from others can further establish your subject matter expertise.

Having a lively comment area demonstrates your audience engagement skills, which are crucial for any writer.

You must dedicate a lot of time and effort to maintaining a blog. If you don't want to do that, consider writing a guest article for another writer's site.

For instance, Make A Living Writing welcomes guest articles to support working authors in their endeavors.

Improve Your LinkedIn Profile

As soon as you finish reading this post, if you don't already have a profile on LinkedIn, do so. One of the most significant venues for a professional ghostwriter to use is this one.

Your first step should be to identify yourself as a ghostwriter. Try to avoid just referring to yourself as a "freelance writer" so that it is crystal clear what you do. After that, update your experience description as you finish assignments.

For instance, discuss the areas of knowledge and abilities you are developing. Additionally, this is the ideal location for you to submit articles you have written or often post about other pertinent information for ghostwriters. Just be sure to convey your experience using general words; avoid mentioning client names or obvious facts about the job you've completed.

Congrats!

There you have it, then. Simple techniques you may use to demonstrate your abilities without going against the profession's rules about confidentiality. Pick one and put it into practice right now.

CHAPTER 10

PRICING AND PAYMENT IN GHOSTWRITING

For people and companies looking for written material that hasn't been produced by them directly, ghostwriting services are a significant resource. Ghostwriters contribute significantly to the creation of top-notch content on behalf of their customers, whether it be books, articles, blogs, speeches, or other written materials. Several criteria are taken into account while determining the cost and payment for ghostwriting services.

Models of Pricing for Ghostwriting Services:

a. Some ghostwriters demand a flat price up ahead for their services. The expected project scope, the length of the content, and the intricacy of the subject matter are often taken into account when determining this flat charge.

b. Hourly Rate: Ghostwriters may charge by the hour for their services and knowledge. When the project's scope is unclear or there are numerous modifications and customer input, this price model is appropriate.

c. Word Count or Page Rate: Based on the word count or the quantity of pages, fees are charged. Clients and ghostwriters can reach an agreement on a specified price per word or page.

d. Revenue Sharing: In certain instances, ghostwriters and publishers may settle on a revenue-sharing arrangement in which they share in the profits from the sale of the book or other piece of content rather than receiving a fixed payment.

e. Hybrid approach: To meet the particular requirements of the project and the preferences of the client and the ghostwriter, a hybrid approach may sometimes be adopted.

Cost-affecting variables for ghostwriting:

a. Project difficulty may have a big impact on how much it costs to hire a ghostwriter because of how complicated the topic is and how much research is needed. Technical or specialist issues could call for more knowledge, time, and effort.

b. Word Count or Page Length: The more time and effort required to generate the material, the longer it will take the ghostwriter, which will affect the final price.

c. Expertise and Experience: Highly skilled and well-known ghostwriters may bill more owing to their solid reputations and writing abilities.

d. Timeline: Strict deadlines or accelerated tasks may incur more expenses since the ghostwriter may have to give your project top priority over others.

f. Research Requirements: Projects requiring in-depth analysis, interviews, and data collecting typically have greater expenditures.

f. Confidentiality and Exclusive Rights: The cost may be impacted if the ghostwriter is compelled to sign a non-disclosure agreement (NDA) or forfeit any rights to the material they produce.

Negotiating Payment Schedules and Terms:

1) Before discussing payment conditions, all parties need to have a clear understanding of the project's objectives, deadline, and deliverables.

2) Ghostwriters sometimes ask for a portion of the entire price up in advance as a promise to the task, particularly for larger assignments.

3) Milestone Payments: For bigger projects, payment may be separated into installments, with installments issued after the conclusion of certain tasks.

4) Final Payment and Adjustments: Confirm the date of the final payment and if it contains a clause for any required limited adjustments.

5) To prevent misunderstandings or payment delays, decide on the chosen payment method and currency.

6) Contractual Agreement: It's essential to have a formal contract that describes all of the conditions of the agreement, including payment

information, the project's scope, deadlines, and any other pertinent provisions.

Make sure that both the customer and the ghostwriter are happy with the agreement, the process of negotiating payment conditions and schedules should be open and fair. Successful ghostwriting cooperation requires professionalism, open communication, and a clearly defined scope of work.

CHAPTER 11

SYSTEMIZING YOUR OPERATION AS A GHOSTWRITER

Developing a methodical Ghostwriting strategy Creating a step-by-step method for ghostwriting may greatly simplify operations and lighten the burden.

Here is an idea for a strategy:

A. Understanding the client's requirements is the first step in meeting the client's demands, objectives, and goals for the writing project. Be sure to make the subject, tone, style, and any other special instructions clear.

B. Information Gathering and study: To guarantee that the information is accurate, informative, and interesting, do an in-depth study on the subject. Obtain pertinent information from reliable sources, statistics, and data.

C. Creating an Outline: For the writing endeavor, create an organized and detailed outline. Organize the article's major ideas, subtopics, and general structure.

D. Writing the First Draft: Begin writing the first draft based on the research and plan. Maintain the ideal tone and style while concentrating on efficiently communicating the message.

E. Review and editing: Check the first draft thoroughly for cohesion, clarity, and general quality. Make the required revisions and enhancements to the writing.

F. Collaboration with the customer: Send the revised document to the client for comments and modifications. To make sure the material reflects their goal, work closely with them.

G. Final Draft Polishing: After taking into account the client's comments, make the material flawless and polished. Pay attention to your grammar, spelling, and punctuation.

H. Quality Assurance: Conduct a last quality check to ensure that the material satisfies all criteria and conforms to the highest standards.

I. Secrecy and Rights: Make sure that any agreements for ghostwriting have secrecy provisions and specify who owns the written material.

J. Effective Communication: Throughout the process, keep the lines of communication open and functional with the customer to immediately resolve any problems.

K. Time management: To prevent delays and guarantee the timely delivery of the ghostwritten material, set realistic deadlines for each phase of the procedure.

Time management skills are essential for optimizing the ghostwriting process.

Here are some pointers for productive time management while working as a ghostwriter:

1. Prioritize tasks: List the most important ones and order them according to due dates and customer specifications. Prioritize finishing up important tasks first.

2. Make a timetable: Establish a thorough timetable that allows precise time intervals for

client communications, research, writing, editing, and other crucial tasks. Keep as close to the timetable as you can.

3. Be realistic when establishing deadlines for the various stages of the ghostwriting process. Without hurrying, provide adequate time for your research, writing, editing, and revisions.

4. Break down projects by breaking them down into smaller, more manageable jobs. With this method, the procedure seems less daunting and you can measure your progress more precisely.

5. Eliminate Distractions: Keep them to a minimum when working. To keep focused, turn off pointless alerts, stay away from social media, and designate a specific workplace.

6. Use time management tools and applications to measure the time spent on various activities,

make reminders, and maintain organization.

Illustrations of books

Trello

Asana

Todoist

Evernote

Calendar on Google

Microsoft Will Perform RescueTime

Timer Pomodoro

Clockify

Focus@Will Forest

Keep The Milk in Mind

Toggle

Notion

Noisli

StayFocusd

Freedom Habitica

Slack

7. Set up defined time slots for each work and steer clear of multitasking. One activity at a time

concentration may boost output and cut down on mistakes.

8. Batch comparable jobs: Assign similar tasks to one another and do them one after the other. Write many drafts at once, for instance, or handle client communications during particular times of the day.

9. Short breaks should be included in work sessions to help workers recharge and keep up productivity. Focus may be improved, and quick pauses can reduce burnout.

10. Track Progress: Continually keep tabs on your development. Examine your finished work to see whether you are finishing by the deadlines.

11. Be Flexible: While adhering to a timetable is important, be ready to adjust if unforeseen problems or changes occur. Flexibility makes it

easier for you to deal with unanticipated occurrences.

12. Learn from Experience: After finishing each endeavor, give the method some thought.

13. Determine areas for development and incorporate lessons learned into the next initiatives.

14. Feedback and Continuous Improvement: To pinpoint areas for improvement and further streamline the ghostwriting process, periodically collect feedback from customers and team members.

You may streamline the ghostwriting process and save time and work while providing customers with a high-quality copy by adopting an organized strategy like this.

ESTABLISHING CLEAR GOALS AND OBJECTIVES FOR EVERY PROJECT OF GHOSTWRITING...

Each ghostwriting assignment must have certain aims and objectives if it is to be successful and live up to the client's expectations.
To do this, follow these steps:

✓ Understanding the client's vision is the first step in understanding the client's goal, target audience, and purpose for the content. Having your objectives in line with theirs will assist.

✓ Define the project's scope, including the kind of material needed (such as blog posts, articles, or books), word count, tone, style, and any particular rules.

✓ Identify Key Messages: Determine the main ideas the customer wants the material to express.

This will enable you to concentrate on properly communicating the main points.

✓ Establish an audience persona to better understand the target audience and to help you generate content that is tailored to their needs and interests.

✓ Establish reasonable deadlines for the project, taking into consideration the difficulty of the subject matter and your availability.

✓ Throughout the project, keep the lines of communication with the customer open and transparent to quickly resolve any queries, updates, or changes.

✓ Incorporate input: Be attentive to customer input and ready to make changes to ensure the finished product satisfies their requirements.

✓ Implement a rigorous review process to make sure the material complies with the client's requirements, meets the agreed-upon objectives, and is error-free.

✓ Respect the project's confidentiality and the client's identity if anonymity is requested.

✓ Review and evaluate the project's success by examining whether the aims and objectives it was designed to accomplish were met. Analyze user comments and statistics (if available) to evaluate the effectiveness of the material.

These guidelines will help you establish precise goals and objectives for every ghostwriting assignment and eventually produce high-quality work that pleases both you and your client.

Determining the target audience and the required writing style for customers

Considerations including demographics, hobbies, and preferences should be taken into account when determining the target audience for a client. To get insights, do market research and examine recent consumer data. As for the necessary writing styles, consult the customer to learn about their preferences, brand tone, and message objectives. Maintain the client's voice and brand identity while customizing the material to the intended audience. Ask the customer for input often to make sure the writing style fulfills their requirements.

CHAPTER 12

SUSTAINING YOUR GHOSTWRITING BUSINESS

Launching a freelance ghostwriting enterprise

Three essential elements are necessary for a successful ghostwriting business:

- The right mindset
- The right experience
- The right skill set

1. **Mindset** : You must be comfortable with the possibility that your work may be published under another person's name. For many authors, particularly those used to writing under their names, this is an odd sensation. Perhaps more importantly, you should feel comfortable asking for a fair price for your work.

2. **Experience**: You don't need previous experience as a ghostwriter to start your own business. However, it's crucial to demonstrate that you possess the following skills: writing experience, customer management expertise, and the ability to handle delicate or private material. Because a ghostwriting endeavor involves more than simply producing material. Additionally, you will be responsible for gathering stakeholders, conducting interviews, doing additional research, and managing corrections or modifications. You must show that you are capable of handling that kind of task.

3. **Skill set**: You need to show that you're competent in interviewing individuals and writing on a range of topics—two things that are important for success in the ghostwriting market. You should include this content in your freelance writing portfolio to make it easy for prospective clients to understand your work.

What not to do as a ghostwriter

Four of the worst faults freelance ghostwriters make include:
- Expecting credit for their work
- Accepting every job offer
- Bragging about customers without permission
- Not having joy in your work

1. **Don't expect credit**: You're paid as a ghostwriter not simply to generate material, but also for your client to control the rights to that content. Legally speaking, you don't own the work you perform for clients—it's theirs, even if you developed it. So if you anticipate credit for your job (and demand that of customers), you are setting yourself up for failure. Most customers don't want to deal with ghostwriters who expect credit for everything, as that's not how ghostwriting works.

2. **Refuse every offer**: Knowing your target audience and sticking to them are key components of branding. You risk damaging your reputation if you choose the incorrect clientele.

3. **Do not boast about your customers without their consent** : Even though you may not want credit, boasting about clients you've worked with is a significant mistake. Many businesses and people engage ghostwriters to create material that they will later promote as their own. It might be detrimental to the reputation of a customer to boast about the job you have done for them. In that case, you put yourself in a position where others will avoid working with you for fear that you'll "blow their cover," to use an analogy.

4. **Always be proud of your work**: It's a common assumption that because your name isn't on the work, you shouldn't give it as much thought.

You can show that this is false. Every ghostwritten piece of content has to be written as if it were going to be published under your name; emphasizing quality, narrative, and attaining the desired result.

Although you are working for a client's objective result rather than your own, your degree of effort should be the same.

Not usually a ghost, but always a writer

A wonderful career choice for independent authors is ghostwriting. You get to engage with some extremely fascinating (and sometimes difficult-to-reach) individuals in addition to earning money. It's not either-or, however; you may work as a freelance writer on other projects as well. The secret is to balance the personal branding component of it. If you become well-known for your work, brands may want to capitalize on your reputation. That's okay if you're aware of it (and being paid for it), but always be explicit about the kind of work you're doing before entering into a contract.

CONCLUSION

When a book is ghostwritten, an author, referred to as the ghostwriter, creates it on behalf of the credited author. Collaboration, clear communication, and secrecy are essential to the process.

Without necessarily having the time or writing abilities to write the book themselves, ghostwriting enables those with compelling tales or expertise to express their thoughts. It is a crucial service that aids in providing readers with a broad variety of tales and information.

It's crucial to remember that ghostwriting makes sure the finished book accurately matches the voice and writing style of the author who receives credit, keeping the story's authenticity and cohesion. Ghostwriters sometimes contribute quietly and without recognition, which may be both gratifying and difficult. Collaboration between the ghostwriter and the acknowledged author, as well as their capacity to construct a gripping and memorable tale that connects with readers, are key components in the success of a ghostwritten book. In the literary world, ghostwriting generally plays a vital part in enabling the sharing and enjoyment of a wide variety of ideas and tales by a larger audience.